Bare With Me, I'm Terrible With Names

by Lian Waite

Because Its Thursday Publishing
2015

www.becauseitsthursday.com

Copyright © 2015 Lian Waite

All rights reserved. This book or any portion thereof may not be reproduced or used in any manner whatsoever without the express written permission of the publisher except for the use of brief quotations in a book review or scholarly journal.

First Printing: 2015, B

ISBN 978-0-9966837-0-8

Because Its Thursday Publishing

www.becauseitsthursday.com

To contact the author send an email to becauseitsthursday@yahoo.com

First Edition.

This book contains material from *Born Ugly* (© 2010) by Lian Waite

This is a work of fiction. Names, characters, businesses, places, events and incidents are either the products of the author's imagination or used in a fictitious manner. Any resemblance to actual persons, living or dead, or actual events is purely coincidental. Don't be vain, that wasn't about you.

This book is not intended as a substitute for the medical advice of physicians. The reader should regularly consult a physician in any and all matters relating to his/her health and particularly with respect to any symptoms that may require diagnosis or medical attention.

to the people who believe in me.

Bare With Me, I'm Terrible With Names

Dear Reader..9

Bare With Me...11

I'm Terrible With Names...87

About The Author...152

Index...154

Acknowledgements...157

Dear Reader,

      This is merely a collaboration of writings. It is not one single body of work. Please do not treat this in such a manner. Take your time reading each poem, each line and phrase. True, I sat and wrote some of these almost as quickly as you are able to read them. Some, you will notice, are left unfinished and purposely so. Some others took years to develop. Some of the things written have taken pain and heartache to manifest. Some come from the happiest moments of my life. Some are completely made up. All parts of these works however have been written under the influence of something, be it love, drugs, happiness, sadness, contempt or content. Do us both a favor throughout the next few pages of your life's journey and pay attention to it all the best that you can. Read a few poems at a time and put the rest away for another time, maybe even another day. You won't relate to everything written and I honestly hope you aren't able to because I don't myself. If you read something that you don't like, don't worry it's not the end of the world, just the end of that poem. Remember also that in order to keep the purity of some of the pieces within, some errors remain. Please again bear with me in this regard also. I appreciate your time, love and patience and I hope you enjoy.

-L.W.

Bare With Me

No Working Title

The day is going to come where I no longer find pleasure in things.
A day will come where I no longer do things for the sake of fun.
A day will come where I'm just merely too old to enjoy life.
On that day I ask, with scrupulous sincerity, that you will find the most violently raging river known to man.
When you find this river, my only other request of you is that you will roll my casket over into the wildest raging, deepest part.
...I've never been to the rapids.

Tokyo Grey

The sounds of the sun kissing earth,
the sounds I hear aren't what they once were.
Twice I heard in her the sounds of heaven above,
as good as she looks in nothing, she looks better in love.
She looks better in me, in this mirror on my heart.
...she's heard blue far too long, and she misses
Pleasure...inconsistent but consistent at being just that.
Pleasure, she gives me, so consistent in fact.
She lives in me, deep. Somewhere forgetfulness can't visit,
somewhere I can't reach with a sea of tears...she lives.
...she's tasted red far too long, and she misses
smiles. Far away, but much too close to be seen.
Smiles, she buys from me with cheap jokes.
We'll speak, and I'll swim in her thoughts for years,
bathing in a love this pure, this unformed, this true.
...she's lived black far too long, and she misses
love...but a glance away it is years out of sight.
Love, I hold onto her hold onto me with love.
We wish, we dream, we hope, we pray
because we know where we go we want to stay.
...she's been yellow far too long, and she misses
courage. The bravest of them all but so unsure to try.
Courage. The will in her might die...
but not if I might have my way, I'll love her all my days.
What I see in her is so great. That...
...Tokyo Grey.

Greener Pastures

we guess its instilled in the minds of this generation
that feelings must be generated, here's the problem.
she was raised in a project apartment
and from the table of love, she was too early pardoned.
distant and dissed, this just a short list, very early on in life she was already hardened.
born to a young mother who didn't want her, she gave her cold shoulders and cut her no slack.
in middle school, new stepdad, he raised her on her back.
high school failed her, she said she's never going back.
moved to one room shack, on the street by the tracks.
flashlights, no heat she would sleep on the floor because its more to afford a new bed than Jordans.
of course, its a course that you crash in or born in, boring is life when losing just seems sworn in
black eyes from her boyfriend, who found out how she keeps the dick coming in and the money too
no secret what she would do...
to afford her Louis Vuitton, Gucci and Prada couture she was having flown from Cali'
and on her feet when she walked the streets she had shoes from Bally
one night left raped in an alley, bruised and beaten badly
next day just as nothing had even happened
fast forward our subject nine months, two sons, no daughter
one's named Jesus because he'll never meet his father
she drops the other off at daycare, no space there in her one room shack for Jack.
she waits, stares, wipes off fake tears because she knows that she's never coming back.
she was birthed off luck and then raised off living.
crying to herself because she never got a whipping.
nobody cared...
and nobody was there to comfort her soul when she was down and scared.
ten o' clock news previewed something that was late breaking...they feared.
no note when she died, just the Savior was there.

David the Goliath

The best thing I've ever done was say "I can".
Even meaning it from the heart, I'm a man...
Not excusing myself, but excuse I hold.
Every excuse I spew, excuses grow too old.
So I'm using my tools of screw ups and loose nuts
to bolt to your life and screw up your loose nuts.
To teach you best from my mistakes, that's the best teacher.
I send the memo to you, hoping my excuses reach you.
I'll tell you things like, never follow a woman,
but if she ever needs you, let her know that you're coming...
and never have a regret, and never mess up your credit,
and never ever be violent and never need a cosigner,
and never let em confuse you, and always grow as a student,
and always grow as a person, and love the ones who deserve it,
and if you just get the chance to ever speak on your feelings
don't bottle them bitches in, you'll kill yourself to conceal em.
Keep it real with the real ones, I'm just trying to be real son,
or these words to my daughter, just trying to be a good father.
but be more like your mother, less bad traits that she harbors.
We show you everything bright, but the world is just getting darker.
Baby I'm of the world and I'm only trying to reach you,
the world promises you excellence, I just promise to teach you.
I'm just writing from wrong, it's all coming from memories.
Don't bite your tongue till it bleeds, but close your mouth to your enemies.
There's so much I want to show, and much more I want to tell you.
Don't trust in the unseen except God and the Devil.
Don't you ever worry, I'm David to your Goliaths.
I'll raise you as I can, and watch you grow perfect in silence...
...I could never finish.

Mama Math

Let's take every time you've ever been sad
plus all the times I made you mad
plus every time I made you laugh
now divide them all by half.
Add every time I made you proud
plus every time you called my nickname too loud.
and every time you introduce me as the baby,
now divide that all by eighty.
You had two girls after that you were okay.
You added me last, now you are grey
If your love was a number, I couldn't count that far
then add 2 "Amen's" and a "bless her heart"
Now take all of that and add thirteen.
Put an equal sign and that's Verdine.
I love you Ma.

For Tami

once I caught a cloud and named it after you
i would only pull it out when skies were too blue
when things got too easy
and nothing was too hard
and life ran at full speed
and my batteriees werent charged
and misspelled words all counted
and no horses got mounted
and all chances of life failed
cuz all the card got counted
and when i did not succeed
and the blame was on me
and when i tried my worst
but was the best was my least
i pulled my clouds to cry and use my heart to sing
i used my pain to hide
i used my smile for things
like hiding pain inside
i use my joy for passion
i use my jokes for cover
i swear to write is my passion
i do everything with meaning
i write every song to sIng iL
i write every poem to read it
and every cut is the deepest
i swear i dont know the meaning
outside i sleep where im keenest
and when i walk around i act like i dont care for help
...maybe, maybe i dont know the best
and maybe, maybe i wonr know the rest
but all the rest i've learned so far
puts me in places that ive been hurt so hard
and all the hurt i swear i hyde
swallow it like its formaldehyde
death like judged by 12
in hell i

I Prey

Dear Lord,
Guide my heart,
Guide my mind
Touch my eyes for I have seen the Devil's heart
Oh Lord, it is wicked but it cries for the lives its lost
My tears flow like blood shed
And my heart aches for the lost.
Bless me Oh Lord and guide me.
Each step small, yet as vast as he sight of man.
My heart aches for the lost with tears of gold
These tears sold to aid the pain of the souls.
Dear Lord guide my hand, aid my heart
Amen.

March Eighteen

I cried once...
It was not a tear shed for sorrow of loss.
Not a tear dropped this day for misfortunes nor were these tears due to the pleasures of joy.
I bathed in these tears. I washed my heart in these tears.
Not my heart of the flesh, I washed my heart that hides somewhere in the bottomless soul of this man.
I cried once, and oh did I ever...ha, ha.
I am not allowed to cry from fear of death, so my tears weren't so.
I cleansed my soul so good it frightened me. I didn't cry for any woman i let down, nor was a tear shed for any man I stepped on. My regrets are in my past and my past won't let me cry, so my weeping was not for such.
I cried once, only once in my lifetime. Sure there were times when tears were shed, pain relieved, and tears subside...but not this time. Because oh when I cried, I cried, and I cried.

Mother's Day Poem

once I wrote the best poem ever
one of those perfect kinds
with all the perfect words
and all the perfect rhymes.
I used nothing less than the perfect thoughts
each on the perfect line.
I used my best polished words
to give it that perfect shine.
I wrote for days on end,
trying to find that perfect time.
knowing today was on the way
I made this my perfect sign.
but out of the millions of words I used
I'll leave you a few, I mean em too
"Thank you much, Happy Mother's Day,
I love you.

Part of You

roses are red
sky is blue
that's two reasons
that we love you.
we love you may
we love you might
so you know we love you
day and night.
good parents you've been
to us so long
you loved us whether
we're right or wrong.
you loved us through
the thick or thin
you loved us whether
we lose or win
sometimes we wonder
why do you love us
what did we do
oh, now we know
because we're part of you.

Real Orange Peelings

I had it all figured out, though the movie was long
Soon I had it figured out, why my movies went wrong
Every scene I believed my mind played on the big screen
But it was a trick and my mind was playing that bitch on me.
Every time I pass a mirror and see that it's just I
I wonder to myself in thought why do I always wonder why...
Because I know his thoughts, and no one else does?
And I know his faults, when no one else does?
I know all of his feelings, when no one else knows.
These are my real orange peelings and no one else knows...
What I mean though.
I try sometimes to get through things that I've seen, oh...
How I wish that I could come clean, oh...
How I wish it didn't sound like it seemed though...
It's my job to smile, whenever you frown.
I get paid to be your favorite clown.
But in my favorite world, I'm not favorite now.
Because my favorite girl, I've letting her down.
I remember April fourteenth when the race got started,
In your recollection it was dearly departed.
I never lost him we were racing to those gates
I'm giving a head start right now he's in first place.
That's how I want feel, so please don't step on my orange peel.

Remember

...remember when I signed all of my letters with my pen name
then started doing funny things, I guess that's when the friends came.
remember when I used to write you every single night
now I'm lucky if once a month I can think of something to type.
you used to share how many people were fake, said I should know the difference
I just never paid attention, it's not the motion it's the mention.
Silver Tongue, for a couple of reasons...we were together nearly eleven seasons
I hate to rhyme, but that's the reason
so I pay phone bills waiting for texts bout how you've missed me
instead I get messaged by Alicia, Karen and Misty
at least I'm caring, you miss me? is it too many wrongs to write?
is it too many lyrics from these sad songs I can type
that won't fix the way I left you...sad, sick and alone?
too many "picking up drinks", too little "picking up phones"...
...I mean, they say it comes with every feature but a dial tone
I'm sorry, I mean it...

                                  sincerely, Mr. Scared of Dying Alone.

Today's Date

there's no way my love for this man ever will fade
its been so many years now April 14 is the day
seven forty two I died at heart, as my father went home
at forty three I dropped my tears cause my father was gone
He told me never say goodbye, cause goodbye means forever
I told him "see you later Daddy", we'll meet up later in heaven
I love him dearly, and I've only loved my mother as much
I pray on my life, that's how I feel I keep him in touch.
I wonder if he knows my thoughts, or are my actions to show
And if he does know my thoughts, does he know what I know.
I love him so much I'd never cry due to his death.
I drop a tear at times to show him that I handled my stress.
I know we will meet again with no more struggles or strife
Some want to recognize death Id rather honor his life...

Teddy's Diary

WAKE UP!!!!!!! When is the ambulance coming?
I know I hear it humming, but how long until it gets here?
WAKE UP LITTLE SUSIE!!!!! We can watch the home movies
that you and your friends made the last six years.
I mean, I thought I was your best friend, your buddy.
So, why won't you wake up so I can hear you say you love me?
Through all the bad times I was right there with you.
You'd throw me on the floor when I let nightmares get you.
I know I couldn't stop it when your boyfriend hit you
and I wasn't much help from when your daddy used to "kiss" you
and your mommy wouldn't listen, I heard you say she won't believe you.
and your sister didn't care, I saw her giving you the needles.
and I couldn't go when you got high up on your Horse,
and we both sat and watched your parents fight until divorce.
Then they didn't want to keep you, and you didn't want to stay
but you're much too young to leave, so you didn't run away.
Okay Susie, I promise now, I've learned my lesson
if you wake up for me now, I'll protect you without a question.
I remember when you moved me from your pillow to the dresser,
where we used to talk often, now it's much lesser than better
but my seat up on the dresser gives me good view of the closet
and I saw you take that little pack of white pills from you pocket.
Like the kind your mommy gives you when you just cant sleep at night
But you took a lot this time right before you hit the lights
Now the sun is up and everything is living but your breath
Wish I could have died for you, rest in peace my Susie West.

Helen Back

I'm writing in my journal, "my name is Helen Back..
I've got a piece of shit life. I live in hell, in fact
my heart failed on me, it "opposite of right"
Sometimes I wished myself "the opposite of life"
and when I sleep I dream that all my realities
are really dreams cause it sucks the life out of me
Hurricanes of love leave flash floods of pain
and every season results in the same change.
Men come and go, sun, rain, sleet, or snow
with the same plans, every woman breathing knows.
Sometimes I just remind myself I'm Helen Back
I go through way too much. I've been to hell and back."

A Red Harry

catch me I'm slipping, catch me I'm tripping
catch me I'm falling, don't catch me I'm crawling
but purple unicorns don't eat red koi
and I don't hang wit dead teddy bears no more.
figure I'd waste a bunch of letters in my next few lines
and when its silent I go an' crack my neck two times
in this line, I recite my A-B-C's
don't like my humor, then you can X-Y-Z
C I'm D-E-F and you're R-S-T
G-O-L-D, the ELEMENT-O'-Pee
I got a heart wit letters, by my wife beating hand
and I'm out of place here, like a shark on land
chest cold I'm sick, watch out when I'm limping
cut my right leg off, don't catch me I'm pimping
did you catch it, I'm tripping, I'm high off life
and this picture in my mind is flashing ipod white
lets waste some colors, bet its not hard as it seems
when I dream, they always turn out copper n cream
in my dreams I wake up where its java and green
and swim laps in a pool that be aquamarine
its good enough to pee in, so I'm turning it yellow
Purple Unicorn rides by to gimme a hello
Suicide Red Koi sits on top of his head
And I wake embarrassed, shit I pissed in the bed...wtf?

Graphic Design

our foreign exchange, pour four and change,
but I won't need your phone number
lowercased in my upper room so I won't need to go home with you
my drink's dirty and my mind too, don't watch too hard I might blind you
making memories that we'll forget, she said "hide in me, till I find you"
we roll up when she slows up, she winds down in that cold cup
I take her down till she knows what and I live there till she folds up.
I'm on one and she's on three and I shoot high, I aim to please
her speech slurs and her pulse speeds and her tight grip is embracing me
she speaks out, yea she speaks out, but it's more like she's singing tunes
the moon seems to fill up the room while it's the brink I bring her too
I dipped in till we pass out still high off what was passed out
then we wake up and we go again and we go again till she taps out
and she...

...in my mind

This is a letter to my thoughts
I think I hate you.
My thoughts are deceitful.
The bastards are hateful.
The bastards are playful, they're full of trickery.
My thoughts have nothing else to do so they're tricking me.
There's truth in a lie but every truth's a lie
Or maybe lies are true, what am I to do?
it's like I'm trapped in my mind & I'm needing my soul
But never needing my soul
4th & long from the 30 but I'm needing the goal
Never needing a goal I sit back & deliver.
I put the Pen to Pad, then let it drop & it quivers
Shakes & distributes my thoughts, get em out to the paper.
Fast as I can write em, 10 more might pour in.
I'm full of thoughts when I'm thinking.
I'm full of holes when I'm thinking, several times when I'm thinking
I wished my thoughts weren't thinking.
I've wished my mind was the tomb at the peak of my peril
Thousands of leagues to bury every thought that I herald
Ever I am alone together with my thoughts the worse discerns of me
I knew I never could fought, no I'd rather say fight them
These moments ignite them, write them, I must, so I fuss aloud to myself.
For the moment of relief, they rush out myself, I bust out myself
I live with tears weeping my thoughts
but my biggest fear is that I fear deeply my thoughts.
Can't close these windows, I'll write until my mind bleeds
Composure, compassion are just the things my mind feeds on
My grind speeds on, though the line leads on
Rhyme on, time...or mix my highs & my highs
Try leads to lies, lies lead to almighty failure
You use your thoughts as is, but all mine are tailored
All mine are great, u-r-n the mind of a genius
Sit back, relax & ride with my demons.
I've ruined myself, thought provoking shit is unsettling
I push envelopes. People tell me I'm mettling.
Tell me that I'm going uncharted, slow down the game shit
I don't have time for pausing, my unadulterated thoughts are insane bitch.
I see my tattoos, don't think what I bought.

Step into my mind, now come & think what I thought.
Come drink in my drought, I'm in when I'm out but never back because
My thoughts are everlasting...by far outlasting & easily surpassing the confines of a New Era fitted
I did it
But I was acquitted, very much guilty
But I got off on my...

...in a sad

in a sad, sad world i live without out you
not for long, but just long enough
in my heart i lust for you that I can cuff
for each moment spent apart i start to doubt you
with your beautiful shape and you come from good company
and you keep at least a pint of that good loving to comfort me
never too much you see i swear you're just right
i stay reaching for you in the middle of the night
and you're all natural that's the reason why
with your "S" curved and your single eye
and you keep saying you're pure, well at least I think
come here let me turn you up, can I have a drink?

An Alpine Pioneer

people won't sit beside me on the bus, I'm raw.
is it my cold hard stare, and my grip tight jaw?
so I re-lax my face as I go to sit up,
but I'm wearing all black, could it be a stick up?
memo: shirt & tie for my trip the morrow
"look at his jacket, could his thoughts be hollow?"
am I thinking... clutch ya purse and hold close ya daughter
'cause I ain't got no morals, never knew my father
grew up in the hood, makin money from drugs
in-ar-ticulate, always runnin wit thugs
what's my great expectation? who the fuck is Charles Dickens?
as I go to stand up, here's where the fucking plot thickens
she yells..."I have my mace, and you know that
and no means no, so why the hell don't you step back
I don't have a million dollars in a safe on a yacht
no Mexicans earn a living using rakes in my yard
my whole life's been hard, afraid I might get robbed
I take the bus like you, to my high risk job.
I don't have a cubicle desk, and my child is ill
and I can't afford my rent, or her medical bills."
then I switch my bus, go to the Concorde route
I sit beside a man I noticed wears a Tom Ford suit
so I ask what he does, he says "My name's Jose
why you all in my shit, why aren't you going away
I don't rake up leaves, out of nobody's yard
and I don't stand by Lowes, chasing nobody's cars
and I don't paint houses, or work on my knees
don't call me racist names, I got a couple degrees."
I say "oops I think I spilled some intellect on me
I'm a pair of pants, don't get yourself addressed homie"
by now I'm upset and inside I'm dying here
because everything I see is an Alpine Pioneer.

A Beggar's Requiem

went on a walk one day and saw a man that was needy
He was holding up a sign the first line said "Please help,
next it said "need food, but will work for money,
then the last line said "please, my kid is really hungry"
maybe He was lying, but I couldn't chance the feeling
so I gave a couple dollars as He thanked me and concealed it.
returned that with a nod and walked away real content
never weighing in my mind where that money really went...
years later I lost my Job and lost my house
both my kids died of cancer, then I lost my spouse
then I lost my hope living out on the street
because my life was filled with rain clouds, doubt and defeat.
even had a little sign said "I'm feeling really bummy,
could use a couple dollars, because I'm really, really hungry."
One day I ran into a kid and he said his name was Tommy
he was crying to a picture of his daddy and his mommy.
said his mommy wouldn't leave him but she had to go today
and his daddy would return but for now He couldn't stay.
see his mommy got a job cleaning carpets in the summer,
and his daddy had a job, He was a carpenter or something,
but He had an accident, that's all he really knows and
it happened on the job, He worked at 33rd and Roman.
he said he prayed so much that it made his knees welt
then he showed me this sign, the first line said "Please help...

Cloudy With A Chance Of Thursday

hearing gunshots, but I just can't quiver
I'm drinking like gills are growing from my liver
and oh my god, the Lord knows I'm a sinner
sold my soul, just knowing I'd be a winner
facing misery on every road that I've traveled
explaining to the blind why they'll never cast shadows
then I get a newfound layer in my struggle
its a full time job having faith in my hustle
my motive is about as clear as spring water
fearing for my daughter for the troubles that I bought her
I'm not perfect, surviving on second chances
the Devil's the musician but I hate the way he dances
I fell asleep on the eve of evolution
this stand still guy didn't receive his revolution
swimming with the birds, mind in the sky
near the end of my rope hoping God didn't lie.

Congraduations !!!!

People think I've lost my mind, I say I throw cents...
but I'm sitting on a cloud
...and pennies from the sky are like bullets in the crowd...
that's science for you,
Waite, I'm not finished...I'm flexible like bread ties wit my written
and I'm not so creative, just using what I'm giving...
lets take a pause for a second
I think Thunder is God's dog barking down from heaven
I really think my palindrome is just what hurts me
forward it's D-O-G and in hindsight, the Mercy...did I miss you? I hope not
maybe I should talk about coke rocks, I mean crack rocks
or I should tell you bitches how my gat pop...
pardon my vernacular, I just called myself attracting you ...
so lets think alike
I paint a vivid picture...sit inside my brain while I blink the lights
kind of like describing to the blind man what the deaf hears
but the deaf is he, blind man no hear...
blind man know here, progress is blind have no fear
just walk in faith or take my hand, first step is where we sprinkled the sand...did you catch it?
or maybe He ain't done working on you, got the ratchet...
your whole soul's jacked up
how long you been walking, man, your whole sole's jacked up...switch
I'm not betting on the 'fore, its two dice time rolling seven for the score...
I lost you
I pulled the switch like your mother from a bush that's by the burned tree, I yearn to be....
wait I deserve to be great...
I bid you congraduations, I'm still earning your infatuation.

Breakfast

illegible ledgers, I don't condone thought stealing
fresh Florida orange juice, man I'm top billing.
got the toast for the ones that don't like me, pause
got all of my papers, I ain't breaking no laws...officer
I didn't see you, that's the reason I was speeding
I been drinking, you can smell it, that's the reason why I'm leaning.
I'll keep my two cents and leave my women in bed
I gota butter this bread, I gota scramble these eggs.
yea the eggs of these snakes are the poisonous variety
I've learned to meditate, I'm trying to reach my higher chi
no milk ass haters in my circle I'm wacktose intolerant
nah, I'm allergic. I start breathing hard, then vomiting, purging
Heimlich maneuver on my life, no rehearsing, I'm cursing
burned my ego on the stove, man I want to do a kush up
but my homie tells me no, said curl these 85 shot bottles of Captain
we open that bitch up, drink the whole damn gallon.
lamping, speaking in a sound you never noticed, focused
Daniel-san, crane kick, lotus, Dragonfly Jones when the bass kick
hold it, face it, double chocolate brownie, don't waste it
kick it like FIFA, low top Vans, I'm pacing.
anxious like I'm waiting on a cycle that she's late with.
writing my senator, address it from "A Stranger"
tell him write me back when he think he's gon' change something
trying to get my change up, pockets on danger
not the type to worry, bank account still flamed up.
keyboard clicking, my girl can't sleep so she tripping
move to another room, make sure its well lit in
typing in my study trying to figure what my goal's worth
check back next year, you'll see that that's a cold verse...

Cake

first two lines should be so easy, you just start out with a rhyme .
now compare her to some things, in the next couple of lines.
like a cold glass of kool aid on a hot summers day.
or she's that feeling in your heart when you're about to run away.
you don't have to go too hard, you're just a couple lines in it .
next drop a mean comparison she'll have to think a minute.
say she's as beautiful as sight, you'll have her so full of herself.
man I swear she'll be so full that she'll be spilling on the shelf.
so now you're getting the flow, but you have to keep it simple.
since she knows you love her eyes, compliment her on her dimples.
tell her how you love her hand and need to hold it when you're walking .
tell her something that she said, let her know you hear her talking.
now tell her how you love her hair, its just that sexy way she wears it.
and there's nothing that compares, its why you want to keep her near.
and all her outfits get set off whether or not if she has her purse on.
tell her if she had a bandwagon, then you would be the first on.
this ain't the type of flow you write then go crazy to curse on.
but you can say her ass is nice, to help you drive your verse home.
write it from the heart man, its cookie cutter, easy bake.
I don't even know her and I wrote a poem for her, a piece of cake.

Dieu Noir

..written on a speeding bullet I forge the symbolism swiftly
a quarter past gone, did you miss me?
no Russian, took a minute on my speech
hold the entendres down like balloon strings
red herring fallacist, malicious wounding of the gums
silver tongue fascist, see the changing of the guns
the guards, a God amongst men I am
Lian to the people, never Waiten on a man
a gardener to the world, please pardon my backhoe
so ahead of myself I'm standing in my shadow.

Forever

Uh...the anecdote was cantaloupe, I think she's sweet on me
Trying to get her out her comfort, but she fell asleep on me
Damn...cant wait on reality to go and David Beckham
But they'll hold u like a soccer ball if u always let em
Never...or seldom. Tell me what the fucks the difference.
You get my point just like the shit that's closing out a sentence.
Where's the end? Or better, where do I begin this?
Am I nothing more to you than a name up on a friend's list?
You might be nothing more than one to fill his team out
Yea that car was nice, he just forgot to pay the lien out
Now you're stuck, so you'll just wait till he go get the ring out
He says you're getting fat and you don't own nothing to sing 'bout
You say, nah you're eating so you can get your weight n cake up
And save a little bread cause you're baking a little break up
I'm not a doctor with my words, so ill make my mistake up
Just take in some of my thoughts and call me if you wake up...

Gateway Drug

I talk.....well, with whom I've been introduced with
I've never met a stranger. I have fun with "all my new friends"
and new friends, they like me 'cause I'm different
but that only lasts until they learn of my indifference.
I tell em Lian Waite is a character I created.
that really only shows up when I drink or I get faded
now I don't really smoke, but I'll drink you over a table
and I stay away from Caine, for the time being I'm Abel.
I'll probably only live once, no space here for regrets
and at the same time, I have too much time just to forget
I hear honesty is something to help me with my confidence
So honestly turning 25 is my best accomplishment
Nope I ain't proud of it, never said that I liked it
but honesty gets me through, so honestly I write it
since I'm writing my own story, I'm bout to put a book out
its coming two days after my death so you should look out
or maybe I should... either way I stay consistent
I've managed to fuck up every opportunity given
when I wear my shades, I'm far away from being cool
don't want you in my windows, inside I'm crying like a fool
so let me close my drapes, even hours before daytime
I don't need those creepy crawly friends seeing where my safe hides
or what I'm putting in it, just let me keep my secrets secret
I'm writing this oxycodone prescription at my neatest

The Greight Escape

"One look into the eye of the beast and without question the menacing aura given off by the mere posture speaks words upon themselves. A seat atop hills, while unbeknownst to all, that only moments ago the beast lived as a recluse. Secluded and visited only by the two individuals that dared muster the courage to show their presence in the same existence of it. This beast, have a heartbeat not of its heart but known of the brain, hath not the brain of reason but that of result. And in the same breath should you know that the beast has but one objective and that is its almighty escape from its dungeon-like dwellings into an open aired freedom...but not just any freedom. This beast beckons to be released to lay waste to everything in sight. Once freed, there is little to heed the destructive nature that has been passed throughout generation. The course of the beasts escape having been run, however long or short it may be, there is a restful moment where the beast is most vulnerable. Just like anything else man has come to lay hands upon, this beast has met its match and finds itself a recluse, perched atop hills accompanied by its two cellmates that dare muster the courage to be shown in the presence if only to feel a sort of primal protection. This is the cycle of the beast's life, hidden in darkness with urges to escape and lay waste to whatever the path shall be only to be captured once more. Oh well, until the zipper falls again..."

Jutes For Scenes

see I've never started at the end, but every door was closed the forest all ablaze
and then fire subdued, the doors they all opened and behind me stood a maze
I stepped inside it back first, eyes fixed forward, no worries, I won't look behind
cause the feeling I was leaving was only temporary, my faith guided every stride
turning right to the left once I left the right, I was lost beneath the day, so careless of the night
not a trip or stumble, I was only checking gravity making sure it works, cause nobody's going to carry me
back first I travel as the mud gets thicker, the walls are getting closer and my breaths get quicker
I see all I pass in my reverse role, it's like my mind is getting younger before I'm growing old
and the people that I meet all know me well, there's a story in their eyes, a story I can tell
now the worries that I lost, recollect on my shoulders, my sorrows on my hip like a holster
and all the regrets that I left behind, now climbed up my limbs and found a way in my mind
but I bet you know the deal, I'm not slowing, got my Trust Boots so my ankles aren't showing.
now I feel a breeze hearing sounds that I remember, like arrows for a bow my body starts to quiver
the punch it hits me like I tried to stop a train, release weakness from my heart and then from my brain
walking back first looking forwards insane, dreaming of helicopters all we do is complain.
to give it up I just walk forward like a tourist, but nothings there for me but a fiery forest...

Lecture

with a stroke of pure genius I paint pictures on the canvas of my imagination. no point or purpose to the eye of man, but an all too well known scene to the minds eye of the artist.
with the flick of the brush I create a thought that raises thought and eyebrows alike. though with each passing moment the ink of my idea slowly begins to fade.
with each past moment I paint thoughts of the future, but far from the sense of the action...each painting resembles the past so much that i must present it as such.
with each future painting I present past thoughts of unbelievable genius, stroked upon the canvas of my imagination to be glorified by my minds eye in the gallery of my soul.
with each gift presently presented I paint a portrait of wisdom.
with wisdom being presented presently all the more ease allows my easel to display the gift I presently share.
and with neither being a future recollection nor a past premonition, I simply present my lecture in its purest form.

Mr. Pilfer

right eye blue and other one two
left eye brown other has two, what to do?
look left, right, up, down, cough, spit, smile, frown
ski masks orange, green, brown...you see the shooter?
duck, dodge, scream, shimmy
think of all the pain that the victims go through
then the relief the painkillers give me.
now you have a dollar full of wishes and a pocket full of dreamers
handcuffs and duct tape in a Beemer...
keep your windows down, no crows feet peeking out
roll your windows down, now the whole street's leaking out
jump, Go!!!, run too emotional to keep it in
don't take my advice, I'm not a friend...
eyes on the camera now, smile while the hammers down
tuck it in, hands moving, no time to stammer now
tell it as it happened, tell it as you know it
no need to really tell, your emotions all show it
the eyes of the watcher always seemed to follow you
you lived for today, you never prayed for tomorrow you
know you got it, gun you shot it, bullets you paid for
loaded and robbed it...
but now here's the piper, and he sent a few lifers
your skin is all purple, can't call mister Fifer
you'll get what you give, never more than your word
one nigga found dead, guess you get what you deserve...

Opus Doe

Scantily clad in ragged garments that dare to give suggestion to the frame of their owner. These garments tattered from years of constant wear and wash with subtle frays in the fabric coming from evening slumber, spent face up, laid upon a bed of rock, gravel, clay, and dust. We find our first guest of the evening just as nondescript as the cloth previously mentioned that is called clothing. With lips of stone and skin as brittle as the air is thin, a heart as cold as the arctic and a stare that would send a chill down the spine of even the bravest of men.

As insignificant a character as made be, if even a name be deserved it would likely be as short and sweet as possible to have it hurriedly retrieved from the brain and thrown from the tongue to save one's self from the bitter taste of even the utterance. The dwelling of this character, unbeknownst to most, is possibly in the most common of all places. A place common even as the hind area adjacent to the property of any place of business or residence, so common this place that it is not even fit to be spoken. Because of this oh so common existence coupled with the attire so drab as to barely even earn the title as such, our guest, whose name conveniently evades the banks of knowledge, is quite possibly denounced even as a relevant being in the very place that life was given and lived. With one question only answered by another, the exacting profession of the unnamed that we have chosen to discuss this evening also is just as evasive as a formal introduction in which the name and title are exchanged.

So as much as we are able to see of our guest in only a glance, and with as many conclusions as we are able to draw there is but so much the eye and mind are able to conceive with truth....but alas, before I remove myself from the presence of my newest guest to attend to the arrival of others, I will at least have the decency to jot on this tag **"Doe, J."**

Terrorist

I speak because you can't hear my thoughts I have a writer's voice.
If this isn't in your curriculum, take a lighter course.
My tired horse named Faith, I got him from his stable
To travel on Straight & Narrow, Destiny's my neighbor
I'm lost on Here & Now, and I blame it all on Fate
Directions got me messed up, and Future's going to be late
Past won't leave, Lazy had to visit Fronting
Wealthy stayed home, and Good Luck just isn't coming
I brought along a piece of Determination to swallow
And wash it down with looking back, because Jealousy follows
Good Timing told me, go to Hard Work and run a right
Your destination's Success, go through a hundred lights
You might meet Trials, don't even think to turn on Bailing
And at the fork in the road, no need to merge on Failing
I thanked him for the advice and gave Faith a twist
Now I can do it my way, call me a Terrorist...

Past My Shades

keep trying, I ain't lyin, well I am Lian...
Waite I'm not trying to confuse you, I was born a one time loser
and I know she like when I come from behind like a Hoosier
first name "That Damn" last name "Wordsmith
thoughts fall from the sky like bird shit
and just like bird shit, I get stepped on
my new name is Futon, I get slept on
you laugh and joke, as I stay jobless
cut my braids off, now my fade's high-topless
took my Jay's off, wing tips on Oxford and
check my credentials, IQ on Doctorate
yea I passed, but my degree don't speak right
green and gold's cool, but that black don't speak white
now they claim that race is just the last debate
I say it's not a race if you can't get past my shade
and if I make it in their club, they call me Tu Yung Way
now they made it past my tint but can't pass my age
they can't pass my taste, they can't pass my name
you just might enjoy my brain...
...if you could see past my shades.

3am in Liansburg

Swimming in the Belvi' and Patronin during high tide
Alcoholic attitude, life jacket Mai Tai's
Geese up in my high rise, I'm not trying to share
downing bottle after bottle, I just don't have a care
but that look up on her face will soon be turned into a glare
and at the bottom of the bottle I can see my mama stare
yea I know it's not her place, and I'll never be too old
would've thought the liquor filled me, but somewhere there's just a hole
let me relish in the moment, let me let the moment breath a little
if you tell a bunch of truth then someone might believe a little
walking off the scene, Denzel, yea dramatic shit
pausing for a breath......time to wreak some havoc shit
people think I lost my damn mind, I need a therapist
actually it's not lost, just kind of don't know where it is
I'm thinking at an all time high, I need a parachute
trying to build my rep, think I might need a nail or two
standing on a treadmill trying to run the perfect lap
world on my shoulders and I'm hoping I don't hurt my back
full steam ahead, I'm not waiting for the pace run
saying what I want, looking bad like a lace front
I'm afraid to lose, I'm not ashamed to say I cheat
second place just ain't gonna cut it, I'm afraid to go to sleep
there's no resting for the weary, there's no toasting up a speech
plus I'm fighting for this money, I can't get it if I'm weak
so I sit up in My Town, write a couple lines down
emotional rollercoaster, laugh a little, smile, frown
smile then laugh again, I'm colder than Shaft n kin
changes in my life and I can't control what's happening
...not finished, but I'm tired.

write then, right away

Release my bullshit to the public and the realest i harbour
Tie my emotions with a rope and draw them closer with a marker.
Upset I get, and write problems all down on a napkin
And every next day flush them then down and walk around like nothings happend

By now im ramblin Nd drunk as shit, but noones toldme so
But ima keep my thoughts pushin forward like came toe, Ima read This Shit Later knwing greater words r impossible,
N thought I have,are synical and mindstates illogical lol
nd eloh ells are dumb Nd bitches xspell their names like fishes and I write when im stupid drunk and make thinfs seem like theyre outa my senses, but im into my all fivers
And I win like 49ers and I lose like goodmen do
And I represent that crew
Fuk who knows bout shit debarge, wtf that,gotta do wit shit debarge....ok, wnough typin, imposting this and itsnot cuz I, drunk butmy phine isdumb

Pompous

back to what's expected of me, swimming in Modelo,
I can't lie so being honest girl you lost me after hello.
...but hello... I'm speaking like it's relevant,
am I the asshole? That's so rhetorical, it's evident.
evidence in practice and the practice makes me better.
my insecurities are so secure right down to the letter.
she told me trust in her because that's just half of the battle,
I responded "I work nights girl, I don't even trust my shadow."
so I have to love myself, just can't believe that you would hide it
bastard child heart, everything is just so damn one sided
mad at everything that I seem to blame on someone else.
Hennessy and apple juice sitting on my shower shelf
my imperfections are what make me fucking miserable
the way I live my life, I make the easy shit too difficult,
difficult impossible, impossible the hardest.
so the easiest I have has got me feeling so lethargic.
I don't eat pudding, so my proof is in the mirror,
being proactive has got my face and future clearer.
leaning a little, but still standing on my own three.
knowledge for days, so I'm just trying to be my own me.
playing all the parts, I got cast as the leading role,
support and all the extras, I'm just trying to heal my bleeding soul.
sharper than a surah, still I'm crisper than a scripture.
I'm so into my own self, I'm slicker than a whisper.
blow me in the wind, no metaphors for smoke.
look again like I'm a twin, I'm the synonym for hope.

The Moment

wrapping her eclectic brain around my finger, her heart soon follows
wrapping her spaghetti frame around the beat, the liquor's kicked in
the door to her soul, now the world is gone silent and still
motion pictures flowing through her head, she's unaware

                                            lost in the moment

twist and groove, spinning her web with a level of lies unspoken
with a flick of the hip and a twist of the head, I see the ending I dread
didn't know what I was getting into, now I just know it's not what I want
now I'm up out of my seat, on the dance floor, on that ass like I own it

                                            lost in the moment

reading between the lines, I found myself in that single dance
the one between the devil and his mistress, the one with the sexy stance
now my world is gone silent and still motion pictures are in my head
but I'm so aware, see what I'm doing out here, I take it as an omen

                                            lost in the moment

sweat covers my face, losing my grip on reality the room's still spinning
bass guitars and the snare move me in a way, now the rhythm is winning
swimming in a tune never heard before, with a whore that I loved in my dreams
so I wake myself, I was sleeping in love and I don't condone it…sweating it out

                                            lost in the moment

unwrap my eclectic brain from around your finger, and give me my heart back
unwrap my spaghetti frame from around this glass and tell me where I parked at
its no door to my soul, I need a jacket, my hearts bleeding down my sleeve
somebody point me to the door, ready to leave…don't you know it

                                      yea I was lost in the moment

Thought Process

thinkin bout what I'd do when I got where I'd be
sittin in my Think Tank wit my Cap on I'm free
free to think about all my time goin 'round
my thoughts keep me up, I'm too high to feel down.
forty sum'n moments, every forty sumn'n seconds
i get forty sum'n thoughts, and bout forty sum'n lessons
can you picture that? I'm learnin from what I write
and everything I write is what I'm thinkin bout at night.
still in my Think Tank, and yep, still got my Cap on
armor buttoned tight, you know, the kind that you snap on.
fool proof arsenal of weapons and machines
terrified to go to sleep, so afraid I might dream.
my Tank gotta mailbox, but nobody writes me
so as my heart turns cold all my thoughts go to Icy.
now imagine that. as White as the first snow
all or nothing money thats kinda how my works go.
talkin with myself, with plans to overcome defeat
forty thoughts creepin in, thirty nine for the weak
thirty nine dismissed, but this one i gota keep
thirty nine came bland, so i Gotta keep unique
yea i Gotta pass it on, Gotta make you say wow
in my Tank no Cap, just wiped off my brow
Gotta get it right, this one you'll wana read
i cant Yo-Yo with my thoughts, gotta praise em like a Queen.
now picture that. thats my thought process
imagine what im thinkin when im writing and im stressed

The Breakup

Here, I cannot stay
all of your bills I promise,
I'll pay...bitch I'm out.

Sicks Menits Lian Waite

sometimes I get trapped in my minds eye
I see through the needles head, its fine
no...I mean its fine, it's so acute I barely see
I have a vision in mind but I hardly need it
I have a scope for my mind now it's darker
I don't assume, I draw conclusions with a marker
I have no worries or cares, I live off laughter
we live where laughter and sadness make you madder
I made a hurry of hell, released my bladder
pissed off the Devil I'm back to try my hand
the work of Satan is evil, this here is man
...I take a moment.
I make a thought I capitalize and own it
I take my shades down to my eyes when I am zoning
you see I know it
my ambition is such that I don't know it...but yet I feel it.
I take such pride that one day I'll reveal it...I will unveil it.
Like wedding pictures you'll see em just where I took em
I had sicks menits to live but now I'm fried. Good day,
Warden, unhook him.

Shelf of Steam

Alhamdulillah...mama birthed a leader.
spitting fire strewn like old kerosene heaters.
and my Spitfire shirts hide very clean heaters.
you can take shots at me, I wipe em off...I'm CIPA.
chip on my shoulder that I carry like bazooka.
no crumbs on my floor, I'm cleaning house like loofah.
I hear the sun shines, but I swear I'm no roofer,
so I have no proof of what you make excuse for.
Alpha and Omega from incision to suture.
I'm blasting from the past but I'm faster than the future.
who the hell you think waking up the roosters...you're late.
CNN says by now I'd be crooked, but I'm straight,
gave the first half up, now the other half baked.
so many damn entendres don't forget Lian Waite.
out of place in my skin because my mind's all left
not left meaning gone, but the right's by itself.
not my chin or my treble but I write it with a cleft.
It's not my life but its damn sure the opposite of death.
they say the good die young and the bad grow old
well if greats live forever, I got some millions to go...

Runway 6

I'm too busy working on my goals, I have to keep it up
I drink so I can dream because I know I'll never sleep enough.
I see it all and sometimes wish I had the nerve to speak it up
or speak you up, or call cause I know I want to keep you up.
you keep me up, the way you sit up on my mind thoughts getting heavy
I might need you, but the thoughts of losing time gets kind of scary
and we know some things changed between us, it don't take a genius
to see it, you did some things that I just cant agree with
and I just did some things you never thought I could achieve
so in the essence of my exit I just want you to believe.
and all the moments that we'll share, we'll be one in the same
I tell you bout my darkest secrets but you're still searching for blame
that's right and I don't get it...I pause I think about it, get back to it
drink about it, dream a story, write about it, trying to get right up out it
pure confusion, lie about it, don't want to stroke your ego
we'll be one in the same, no matter how far apart we grow.
You loved me, and I loved that, and I loved you, we loved strange
like big bills we were destined for change, the end all in this love game
we still hold hands, at least hold hearts, and these cold words have warm starts
and these cold thoughts have warm sparks, but this guy here wants no parts...

Giesha

...bermuda short wearer, the I don't care-er
scratch off burning all my gas, and won't spare a
cent on my homies, if I got it I'm a sharer
writing down my thoughts till I'm dead and pall beared up
switching my style once a week for a hater.
but everybody love me, at least to my face.
in my Tokyo denim, forest green innards.
no need to congratulate me, I knew that I was winner
I'm first place, numero uno contender.
step up, get smacked down thinking I was finished.
hiding in plain site, attention span like fish dreams.
Any man looking for me, try looking in your bitch's dreams.
tied down, Nancy Kerrigan, no ice skate.
speed racer, slide across lanes, no ice brakes.
turn one eighties on the fool, achoo.
spew hot soup and lyrics, hoping that you hear it
look past the words, please listen to the spirit.

hisstory

...my dreams of you just overtook me.
I just want you to know, this is not how I thought it would be.
You tried to plead, in hopes that I'd stay.
But I watched you leave, before you knew I'd go away.
You hold my heart, and yet I only touched your sole.
You thought my words could help to heel you in the cold.
All of our moments will be just that...
So, I just wanted you to know that it's all on me.
There was no way the pen I held could help right hisstory.
Now I don't want to be apart, this love just isn't love to me.
If it is easier to assign me a love, that love I'll claim.
If it is easier to cope if I do, then I'll accept that blame...
...but I just wanted you to know,
No I couldn't be, no I couldn't be
No I couldn't live up to hisstory.

"I pray that today is twice as good as yesterday, but at best, only half as good as tomorrow."

Write Up

my cousins keep saying work hard at what you want to do.
and I just keep writing down the shit that I be going through.
guess that's what I want to do, tell you how I'm feeling man.
problems come, but God just keep me spinning like a ceiling fan
and I just keep on sinning man, I'm far away from perfect.
so hold onto your heart baby, sorry if I hurt it.
money changed me, yea I was happy when I had some.
then to dead broke, just as happy when I had none.
both ends of the spectrum, trying to help a dumb guy.
planning for the future, call me Wise Ole' Young Guy.
when I draw my feelings out, all I see is ink blots.
and all the friends I made last year was at the drink spots.
I used to know it all until I wrote it down and burned it.
this wheel is like a tv channel, someone needs to turn it.
and I just want my turn, but I'm feeling so remote.
and my batteries are bad, plus the power button's broke.
so CLAP, CLAP, congratulate the kid that got the goody.
don't want to Buzz around with people plotting like Woody
playing both sides, guess they're trying to save face, ahh
my friends switch and go both ways like racecar.
I'm steady trying to write up, so I can get a write off.
I'm writing everyday now, I'm scared to take a night off.
its 3AM IN LIANSBURG, I'm about to turn my light off,
but feet on their necks, I can never turn my fight off.
they want to bring me in, get me comfy "put my shit down"
I told them how I work so much, I'm sleeping if I sit down
people kicking shit now, I call em Dr. Scholls.
I'm cool man, I take more shit than toilet bowls.
but I could never give the fight up, frustrations going right up
and haters get excited when concentration gets lighter.
So before my mind is gone or my hands get tired,
I'm armed with this pen and I'm gonna make this bitch write up.

Government St & Cherry Ave

Its just me...and once again I'm all alone in this
I swear if being lonely was art I'd be the Van Gogh of this...
but if I could paint it up, it'd be romance, we'd slow dance,
in a slow trance, we'd stare deep in each other's eyes.
you'd tell me lies, about other guys, you'd try and try,
but its hard to hide, with your windows closed, your heart would cry.
you hold so much hurt and have so much pride.
before you let me see it, you'd die inside.
then my hands will grip tight on your side,
and you'd fight them back, but those tears would pry.
and I'd lean to you and you'd wonder why,
and I'd kiss your eyes before you go to sigh I'd say...
...be you, nah I'm serious girl, just be you.
I've been here being myself for a while and my regrets might add up to two.
you might cheat a bit and might lie a lot.
and be tough as nails, but still cry a lot.
no matter how life goes we only do it once
just to let you know you can't die a lot.
...then take you to my room, do a little damage.
I talk dirty, you speak Spanish, you say I can't take it.
I promise I'll manage, body so preserved got me here trying to can it.
I swear...I'd be like Michael Phelps in that ass
that's how I would draw it up but apparently I got an F in art class...

The Last, Last

at your best, be the worst. it is as okay as the sunshine.
write your favorite song with every word you speak.
let every joke be the worst joke you've ever told.
enjoy your beautiful home and family.
cry when that door gets slammed in your face.
write me when times are good...
call me when times are bad...
smile when you think of me,
call when you miss me.

Photo Racers

Wherever you live, live free.
Grab a cloud, and be with the winds, if they will have you.
Live not with man...never tame that free spirit.
Be a spirit driven by your own will and as free as the fires of hell

It's a New Year

...and on my life I plan to write it in the best fonts with an expensive pen on the best paper made. I woke up thinking I had to go to work and after I realized I had the day off I was just thankful I had LIFE in me to even go to work. I won't ask anyone to take me serious because I know I make jokes a lot, but I will ask you to take yourself serious. Enjoy this thing called life and don't take it for granted because you only get one shot at it. I plan to laugh more this year. I hope I can experience something so wonderful that I'm moved to tears. I'm open to love. I believe in a God and I'm thankful for the opportunities afforded to me but I know I have yet to reach my full potential. I ask you again, because it's important to me, to take advantage of the time you get. SHOW someone everyday that you love them. Find something new to appreciate each day. Fall in love with something and/or someone all over again. Do something you never thought you could. Scare yourself with success. Don't do it because someone else said so though. Do it for you. Sorry if this isn't what you expect from me, but I'm probably not what you'd expect me to be anyway. God bless you and I hope you get more than anything you ever dreamed for in the future.

Within

If my sight is not, how shall I understand red?
If my hearing is none, how will I know what is said?
If my speech has yet to grow, how will I tell what is said?
I want to feel what is within
To share what has been...
There is only time between us and that has not been
This time don't bring to light what has been
Because this is not been yet.
I want to feel your heart
But I want to feel you from within,
Please don't wash me from your skin
do this all from within
As much as the thought has arrived,
Arrive next from within.
Come with me, come to hear her with love
If it's fast enough I will let you win.

Work

pull out chairs and open up doors
call her for nothing, not bitch, not whore
give him a hug, and kiss him goodnight
teach them good things, raise your child right
work everyday never call in sick
and if "C"'s are all u muster, work hard don't quit.
don't plant a tree, plant a forest
no indecision, be the surest
without a blemish, be the purest...
and if u need some reassurance.
pray to God until u cry.
laugh at jokes like u might die.
don't ask "who", stand up, say "I"
say "because I can", when they ask "why".
give from your heart and not from your pocket
and love who you are or else just stop it.
you see, life's not that short so u have plenty of time
to work on your work and live a life that's fine.

Chance

I stand to tell you that he is worth it
Sometimes that minute is good enough to spend
Sometimes that name is good enough to remember
Sometimes these tears will forget to flow
Sometimes that love is genuine
Sometimes...
Be tired of waiting as such as you have to
Sometimes you have to take it
The choice to say sometimes you love.

Blank Canvas

She loved he
And he is me
And I loved she
For what she never meant to be.
For reasons unseen
She lives in my dreams
Though I know it's unclean
I accept it.

Henry I Valentine

girl you look good won't you come a little closer
let me put your back against the wall like a poster
all my friends call me Hen, but you can call me what you like
we'll be friends till the end all we need is one night
or, one day date, lets make a play date
before we get it in, girl I want to phone a friend
no matter how I give it, yea I'm sure that I'ma win
then we'll be so close, we'll take pictures, we'll make toasts
we'll be the life of every party, just get close and get it started
inject me, dissect me, ingest me I digress
see the moral is this, that every story is this
told from point of views, and I'm notorious
cause now I got your body and I'll steal your time
no need to hate me now girl you're running out of mind
and the way you get it back is to pass your love around
that's right, have us running rampant, the best swingers in the town
that's why I love you, now I don't need you
body and mind will soon start to deplete you
and I don't like it, I don't love, I don't need it, I cant fuck with
you, like that, its true cause like that, I'm so charming only few can fight back
fuck up your life, fuck up your demeanor move and change my name to Allen I. Dream Sr...

Heroes & Heroine

...everything I thought I loved was a facade,
friends going undercover on me, Israeli Mossad
maybe it was all my fault to fall in love from the start,
would have killed for her
love like a holy war, Jihad.
lets put that blame gun down, some things I know I like to dream about
and go to all those places that important people sing about
she told me she would wait forever,
 guess forever came a week after I left her
I guess it's cool, now I see that I was wasting my efforts
worst thing, I wasn't gone far, I just took a vacation
she molded my heart into a footstool...claymation
all the things I had to say when I came back,
doesn't matter so much, it's not a shame in me saying that
there's no light in my tunnel, I'm loneliest in my heart
and even my shadow leaves me alone when it gets dark
I gave her that hero love, I swear to God I was super in
but that was just another game of hers I was losing in
and this is not about the one you're seeing in the mirror
so wipe those smudges off and check your face out even clearer
vain bitch, it feels good to you, just like I thought it would
I'm sure you're doing better than I ever even thought I could.

Oui

yes, we are...but what are we? who are we?
we are the ambitious trendsetters
we are the unforgettable go-getters
we are much less than perfect
we are much more than worth it
we are much less than what we have the potential to be
we are much more than 40 ounces and weed
we make the best friends and become the best spouses
we throw the best parties because we live in glass houses
we never fall, never falter, never fail
we never lose, we never win, we never tie, we never bail
we always trust in the first lie that you ever tell us
we are never insecure, we never ever get jealous
we care way too much that you won't have a care again
we are you neighbor, family member, friend
yes, we are...but who are we?

Young Love

Riding in my whip, on my way to see my Shawty
Walking in the door, cant wait to get it started.
Checking in the fridge, whipped cream for the party
I'm gonna take care of my woman tonight...
Got the lights dim and I'm singing slightly off key
I can't get her off me, I'm hooked like coffee.
Heart 'round her waist, and my hands kind of offbeat
The girl is so soft, body sweet like toffee.
All her friends wonder why she still hasn't lost me
I'll give her the world no matter what it cost me
Spend some time wit her, and I might let her boss me
I'll take care of my girl as long as she don't ever cross me
Got her throwing pillows on the floor and trying to toss sheets
Take her from the bed onto the floor, she get the top seat
She sounding like she want me all night
It sounds so sweet
Now I want to put my effort in it....

da Vinci's "David"

...it probably weighs on me way more than it should, but I understand you. You're an artist, you're amazing and you love to create.
I can see the masterpiece that you're creating with your heart. I can see the sculpture that you're having created by all the love and pain that you put your heart through.
You're a good one, you.
No, seriously. I see it now...it's not that you don't want to be hurt, you expect the hurt.
You flourish in the pain, you thrive in it, it makes you a better you.
You know all too well that you couldn't give me your whole heart, not yet, it's not ready.
That's your masterpiece.
You gave your whole heart once and it got broken, and that's when you started sculpting.
That's what it took, that first chip. So now you've come up with a plan.
I see it too.
I gave you my all, foolish child that I am, I gave you all that I had and you knew better.
You've learned from the past so you gave me a piece.
You know that if you lose this it only helps create the sculpture so you know how much you can spare.
We both know you're only hurting us to create art. Magnificent art.
We both know it'll never work for us this way. I told you that if you won't give us a real try that it'll never work. You said you're afraid I'll hurt your whole heart, but we both know better. You know you'll lose this piece that you gave me because I can't survive on a piece of you.
I can't survive because I'm selfish and I thrive on effort. Fucking society.
...but society can't help you perfect your art.
We knew the day would come and as expected we don't last, but your art only gets better. Your heart may lose a chip, but you knew that chip needed to go to help perfect your masterpiece...
Your "Atlas".
Your "Christ the Redeemer".
Your "Thinker".
Your heart aches constantly, but you stay the course because dammit you know what's worse. You know love hurts. You can see how hurt works.
You just know that you're closer. You just know it's almost over. You smile because the end is nearer. You can see the outline of your artwork clearer.

Chip, chip away. Heartbreak, one after the next.
One mans mind and his sex. One step more in your past. It's not heartache, it's a cast.
So you work and you hurt, and you give up a chip.
Just to lose it because love takes a bit more than this.
Yes, you know what you know but you've made up your mind, that one day oh one day indeed in due time. You'll complete this piece.
You'll complete your masterpiece and reveal it to the world.
...just like da Vinci, yes, like da Vinci. One day when you're old and you've lived life a plenty you'll comb through the history books and you'll revel in the glory of his works.
Then you'll take a step back to admire what you've accomplished.
You'll sit back and realize that through years of chipping away at your heart through error after error that now you've created a masterpiece...a "David".
Yes, just like da Vinci.

Be More

...and they're known to leave you hanging
they'll take and take and take
then turn and ask you why you're angry.
I'm just sitting here praying for my brother and his hopes
he's telling me how he would rather riot than revolt.
I know he rambles when he smokes, but I listen to his speech
he says "apparently it ain't shit for me to get cut down in the street,
and left out in the heat, like strange fruit off a tree.
I'm finding it harder to believe, when the wicked are roaming free
protected by some official that they say was elected by me.
and I refuse to go to school, 'cause dammit college ain't cheap
and my children gotta eat, plus I can't afford the time,
you should know something else, those history classes don't teach mine,
and if I define cosine it won't help me get hired where I applied,
so if I get killed on my hustle at least I'll die saying I tried."
...and we talked for about two hours.
They can't take away what you've learned, let that be your super power...

3/5

I hope for great nights and better days to make one
opportunities are plentiful so I will take one
to pray in the light and let feelings flow from my heart
because even my shadow leaves me alone in the dark.
my ignorance precedes me like a foraging pilgrim
but natures contradiction is my unheralded wisdom.
This definition of success in everything that I address
but unbridled intellect is all that I possess.
I don't wish to be rich. I'd rather live forever in script
Just as quiet as a picture amid unresolved conflict
Relentless intuition, to understand what is missing
is to make full commitment to discard the cards you're given.
She claims to believe in the future, but what does that earn her?
Will she die for her beliefs to be remembered like Nat Turner.
Would you rather be a carbon copy or carved from a rock?
See, I want my words to have power like, say, a Haile Selassie.
...the revolution will be televised, it was narrated by Gil Scott
directed by Spike Lee, and scored by Hip Hop.
starring a man, for names sake we'll call him Tyrone
and systemic belief is that this all begins in my home...

I'll clear my schedule and never come up missing to you,
if it'll help your soul to have me sit and listen to you.

Mood

Stand up.
Climb.
Climb feverishly out of your boxes.
There are matters at hand that need your fervent attention.
Stop taking guilt trips claiming that your soles hurt.
Opportunity in your hands with you not aware of it's worth.
Generations set free by a compassionate King
And the only thing we're guilty of is having passionless dreams.
The passion, it seems, it flashes, it seems, in splashes, it's seen.
A people obsessed with selfies, yet they're lacking esteem.
Get hot and get steamed.
So often it seems that I'm asked to believe and trust hard
...but even my shadow leaves me alone in the dark.
It gets harder than hard and harder to find things to believe.
With so much strange fruit cut down from my family tree.
Question anything.
Question decisions. Are these solutions?
If there is a question of motive then those questions can ruin.
Question attention, then question intentions and dig deep.
Quick question, is a shepherd still a shepherd without his sheep?
Make success your cologne.
Make sure you reek of revolution.
Make sure your steps are sure and free from pollution.
...and then stand up.
Climb.
Climb feverishly out of your boxes.
...because there are matters at hand that need your attention.

Monedays

Lets begin with a belief in what I seek, and I seek freedom
from my own depravities no place where I should lead them
I sit and watch, being much more costive than cautious
and claiming what I have to be gifts, knowing damn well what I've lost
is much more, and much more valuable than what's at hand
I've accepted my own lies and excuses because I am man.
No, I won't claim man, I must say that I am flesh
and bone and if we split words you may suggest that I am blessed
I must digress, though in theory at times I have impressed
and anchoring my stress is when I gave much less than my best
now it is all just another test for this orb inside my chest
and I will regress unless I wrest what's left of life from death.
I move with grace differentiating betweens idioms and dreams,
still learning friendships and affiliates and the differences between,
with my unexplainable inconsistencies, how can I lead a team?
It's like I'm sitting with a blind man and asked to describe green...
(to be continued)

titled

growing up I feared snakes and being average.
you see, them snakes sleep in your grass down to kill you for your talents.
within my words I stock my bond, just like you need a check for balance.
and the fear that I might fail's gonna work me 'till my soul is calloused.
Now I know I attract her because I'm driven
There's no time to think of death, because I know how I'm not living
wish I had a dream that I could sell ya, if you needed I would help ya
I'd trade my dollars for sense, but that don't mean that I'm not a failure.
Mediocrity heals the world, or at least it seems so.
and I know that you're gonna shoot me down, so what the fuck am I having dreams for?
If I let you tell it, my first try might be my last,
and if I let you sell it, the only diamond I get will be dusty glass.
I keep unwrapping this shaky present trying to leave a perfect past
when it's on me, no alarm clock, if I fall short of my task.
So I know if I work smart, don't desert God then I'll shine bright like the sun
I mean if I work hard, I deserve all that I get cause I'll only get one dream...

The Silence of Forever

Allow me to explain my brain, my thoughts,
and the things that I do to maintain.
I wasn't born to a silver spoon, no trust fund to gain,
no diamonds or gold chains.
Yea I was born to handcuffs, shook em off.
They paint a picture of me wit handguns, took em off
the wall and boxed em. I make a better picture wit my pencil n pen,
so away I locked them.
A sometime Republican,
Democrat's don't fuck with, Independent who learned game.
Who wants to help the bloody,
but all the people wit money point to us, who they in turn blame.
While they in turn claim, that they in turn changed,
so they can turn change into what's best for us.
And I don't want to hear their bullshit,
so instead I pull shit into my motto, success or bust.

See I don't know about conflict diamonds,
the conflict that I know bout is constant trials.
The conflict in the constant is varying change,
if it's one thing people fear then it's carrying change.
Not the coin for the barter, but the choice for the martyr,
the leader of the peers, the Order over the Charter .
This here idea's harder, than following dreams.
It's like sitting wit the blind and trying to describe green.
Have you ever pictured what a man goes through to give him reason to
believe that he wants to be a leader?
The product of his pain and his pleasure,
added to the ability to speak and make you a believer.
Or maybe he's a born one, naturally so,
handcuffs shaken off to help his passions to grow.
And if actions are to only way to know,
the way I feel I vow to forever let my opinions show...

Dear Woman,

Do not believe that you are anything less than amazing.
Do not conform.
Do not fold.
Bend if you must, but only at the knee.
Do not set yourself ablaze trying to keep warm this cold world.
You are this world and it lives and breathes through you.
You are the creator of Kings and the ruler of nations.
You are our mothers, sisters, daughters, wives, lovers and friends,
but most of all our equals.
Love yourself, because you come first.
Love your sister, because you know her struggle.
Love us, because you know we need it.
I admire your courage and I envy your resilience.
God bless you.

-one man

Woman

She was not a wife,
  and that did not bother her.
She was not a mother,
  and that did not faze her.
She was not the overwhelming
  object of any man's affection.
She was fine with that.
She was love. She was life.
She was pure. She was woman

A Piece of Quiet

She is of the world
Therefore she shouldn't be tied down.
Loose her reigns.
As a breath escapes only to return, so shall she.
Loose her reigns.
She is the world. She represents peace.
A piece of quiet. A piece of love. A piece of heart.

Her.

Her mind breeds indecision, Her goals are too far to crawl
This all proceeds inhibitions, so she'll wait for a star to fall.
Her eyes weep in tradition, so used to the pain for so long.
So hard to keep Her ambition, so she settles for things that come.
Her breath is lost with constriction, she won't put up a fight for more.
Too focused on current conditions, to know what the fight was for.
Her heart beats with submission, afraid of the world she knows.
Blood flows from the incision, some scars just won't heal on their own.
Her soul suffers malnutrition, so long since she's lost Her self.
She counts her blessings and omissions, yet Her crown remains on a shelf.
Her hands carry her suspicions, she's afraid she can't trust all alone.
Afraid she'll bring into fruition, every fear that she's grown up to own.
Knee deep in intuition, so sure she'll have no way of escape.
Steadfast in this position, she thinks that being complacent is safe.
Feet worn from expeditions, she'll kneel she's in no shape to walk.
Her life's filled with indecision, so she'll wait for a star to fall.

I'm Terrible With Names

Snow Days

i hate you...nope, nah i fear i do

i mean i trust you though, i really, really, really swear i do

i blame you blame me for it all i can't help
i mean i can change but i can't change myself
i got feelings that i know you don't know about
i know i have things that i know, that you know i don't feel a doubt
i tied my own blindfold and i walked the plank
i wasn't over water, you just took me to the bank
i know you're not worth it but it's better than hurting
i know halfway down that aisle it'll all turn to perfect
i write what i know cause i know that i deserve it
i know you know you don't want to be deserted.
i'm not about to let you see me get emotional, i'm not really sad
i seem to have replaced my good days with my bad
i have a bag full of moments
i have a life full of fears
i had a loving wife, but now an ear full of tears
i don't miss what i had, i miss the everything that i was
i wish i did it all over just because...
I love you.

Converse

Her heart beats a tune,
I'd sing to.
Her love has a string,
I'd cling to.
And I won't relent,
I have to.
To rise from the fire.
To give her my life to have...
Today.
Sometimes my arms
miss her.
Who can I hold?
I need her here to love,
I need her warmth, I'm cold.
Sometimes I can't
miss her.
I'm cold.
I don't want her here to love.
But I need her.

Monday Origami

It's her unintentional beauty.
Maybe it takes her hours to prepare...
...but it looks like she doesn't really need to try.
From here I stare, wishing and thinking.
Hopelessly in love with a woman I barely know.
Maybe it isn't love, but damn it feels good.
Dreaming of her. Thinking of her constantly.
I watch the way she walks and I notice the slight dip in her hip.
I notice that when she talks she smiles then bites her lip.
And I want to tell her about these things because I
want her to know how much I care. I keep wishing...
Wishing I could wake up in the locks of her hair.
The smell of her washing over me each day.
Every morning waiting to see her open her eyes.
Maybe this really isn't love, maybe I should give this up.
But what if I don't? What if I go for it?
She works weekends, I'm off those days.
We can talk at night...all night, about things.
About the universe and she can teach me about the stars.
I can learn so much from her, I just know it...
but I'm too afraid to go for it.

Poems & Songs

she wants to come for my heart, I just can't bring her along
she reads my poems and songs, and I'm just left with my wrongs.
she's always looking to love, she's always looking for peace
but at the end of the day, wish she was looking for me
I'm everything that I am, but that's still nothing she needs
she wants to give me her heart, degrees of pleas till it bleeds
when I look in her eyes I can see clear to her heart
and every time that we finish we end up back at the start
she wants to come for my heart, but I can't bring her along
she's left with poems and songs, that's just me writing my wrongs
she knows I cheat and I lie, and yet she still loves me to death
she says the way she sees it, two wrongs won't make three lefts
she screams till she's out of breath, and her throat feels like its strep
she claims that she's at her best, but I know her hearts a wreck
she wears the smile of a clown, she feels she's permanently down
and the weight on her heart just couldn't be measured in pounds
I give her poems and songs 'cause I can't right all my wrongs
windows of pain that I watch, just see me coming along
I fight with faults that I have, though I can't trade in my fears
wish I could sell her a smile but she'd probably pay me in tears
I drink it all till it's gone, just can't be sober or sane
only thing worst than a hangover is the thought of the pain
...I drink when I'm high...I smoke when I'm low
either way I can get away, that's the way that it goes
I gave her poems and songs, now I'm just writing my life
one thing that she'll never be to me now is my wife
we went right through the good and never cared for the pain
holding the weight of the world and never thought of the strain
she tells all her friends how much she's single and proud
but she knows that's only true while she has people around
she wears her sorrows around like kings wear a crown
with all the secrets in silence God knows she won't make a sound
I'm kind of wishing I never wrote her a song
and kept my poems for me
sorry to string you along
wish I could cry all your tears, wish I could take all your pain
but if its back to the good, wish I could have you again
I'm far from who I should be
I see the man that you want, and that man just isn't me

all the time you waited for me
a work of fiction this is, but you relate so to speak...
we wished on every star in our sight
I wrote you poems and songs and then I told you good night.

"VI."

I pour my soul in a glass.
And I hand it to you.
You know just what's in your grasp,
I'll hand it to you.
You know all the right questions to ask.
I mean dammit,
Do you know this has to be my hardest task?
It's minor damage to you.
I'm just small talk, time passed,
loose planning to you.
My mind's a bundled wonder,
I try hard to expand it to you.

Driftin' On By

I want to lift you up, but always let you down
the last letter we wrote is my favorite letter now
its been that way a while, about a quarter life
even lower case, that's for your shorter life
I write a poem or two, I know you never see them
I write the perfect words, knowing that I'll never be them
your smile is like a breeze, something that I never touch
but it just makes the day better if only a little much
its all abstract, I know, but you know the reasons
we're spring and summer babies baby, you know the seasons
and the ending of all things, you know of all things
I love you and what we have over all things
I send this open air to you cause it never dies
and I was never lying when I said I never lie
I hope and prey on my own mind sometimes
but I know that we'll be more than less with some time.

First Grade

whatever reason we're apart, I guess is best for us both
though the timing is the worst, I see a vision in scope
whatever happened, that's what happened, it happened and now its over
no need in wishing on the past, because the future is closer.
it seems I loved you as a friend, but wanted you as my own
It's like you lived right in my house, but didn't visit my home.
to tell the truth, yeah I'm jealous, that's something I will not hide
would you believe I've held these feelings deep, down and inside
I can do bad all by myself, I'm good as dealing with stress
I survive things in which I do, because I know I am blessed
I wish my prayers on the world, and all my thoughts for the helpless
I'll never pray for my own wants because I know that it's selfish
I'll never pray for his departure, but I can hope it and wish
I'll simply wait a while and see, cause they say patience is bliss.

Ear's Full of Tears

If my heart had a heart
I'd still be alive
I look towards the light
for a being on the other side
in this final test
I do my best
In the end line of trials
on a bed of roses I lie
ears full of tears
and I don't know why
I have my will and my word
I am lost; so dark, oh so dark
I thought love would find me
But even love is blind.
So I fight to hear
With my ears full of tears
I give this all one shot
I give it all my best.
To no avail or to the best outcome
Either goes or either comes
I fight, I fight back my cries
I hear not
Because I have my ears full of tears
One grand u-turn wont turn it all around
A soldier indeed I am
A soldier with ears full of tears.

The End

How could you let my love overflow?
You were my everything, and everything was in me.
The peak of my life, and the reason for my dreams.
Now I speak silence and hear the sounds of tears
I cry to the clouds because now I have no fears.
I am free now, but the most confined of ever
I have never, ever never said never but now I never
Shall give my heart over
I will end on my own note
On my own blade goes my throat

Burnt Glass

they say you can't steal what's yours to have
that's why I gave you my heart to put it in your bag
you see, I wear it on my sleeve, and my life the same
I love hard for what I want, and I fight the same.
I hear giving up is tough, and trying love is worse
well walking out is easy, losing love just hurts
and if time heals wounds the same as shedding tears
I hope you need to flood an ocean for millions of years.
so never mind my tears, that happens when I see the wind
and the blood on my chest's from where I cut my chin
nothing to do with you leaving, because you found your life
and look at me being foolish, I thought I found my wife
I thought I had written you the most perfect of songs
but my hook was all off and all my verses were wrong
and my key was just shit for all the notes that you hit
I'm big enough to admit, that it's you that I miss...

Bang! Went My Shooter

Was twenty five and she twenty six
We lived life like a bunch of sticks
Together like flash and camera clicks
Until one day her love I missed...

She's gone,
she shot me down.
she's gone,
she took my heart
Bang!
Went my shooter
damn,
I took it hard.

Music played and we danced
A dance of love, that sweet romance
She left the day the music ceased
That same sad song my heart still beats...

she's gone,
I lost my love.
she's gone,
she took my heart
Bang!
Went my shooter
damn,
I took it hard.

This love I've found I need so much
This smile, this heart, this soul to touch
My heart is lost deep in your clutch
Reminding me what I've missed so much.
And when I think of her I'm ashamed
With no one but myself to blame
Thoughts of my journey remove the shame
But the outcome makes my heart go...

...BANG!...she took me out.

All I Want Is You

Raincloud, rainclouds, rain clouding up my judgment
Public displays of affection, oh how I loved it
And loved you, and all the little things that you and i do
I tried to, be good but you still told me bye, you
Never seemed to hurt, would paid to see you try
Said I still want a friend, but we both know its a lie
Now I'm sitting here dying with a pocket full of dimes
And they won't help me buy a moment of your time
Thinking about my last, even sprayed your Chanel on her
Hindsight for glasses, didn't like how it smelled on her
Threw me in the game, wasted my season pass on her
Schooled her all day, but I couldn't push class on her
Passed our favorite spot in the park bout a week ago
Been two years we've been apart bout a week before
Gave me your heart, but I took you for Horace
Trying to save face but now it's not important
You know they say wrong plus wrong is never best
Damn sure don't equal right, so I guess its why you left
Now I'm left here feeling right, yep, right by myself
And I'm way past crying, now I'm crying out for help
See this hole is my chest is really aching like a tooth
And every time I said I love you, I only meant the truth
Used to love sky bluc now its raincloud hues
Cause now that you're gone, all I really want is you.

All Over Diane

I think its funniest lately...
...how I say what I feel, but you twist it to hate me
we're drifting step by step by step, now we're barely relating
and I admit that its on me, it's not a care in me lately
and it's not like I chose to hurt you, it was you that made me
your heart's in trouble now you think you're through with loving
cause the only time we talk is when we're throwing shit and fussing
now you hate the day you met me and you hate the fact we rushed it
and I'm searching at the bottom of this bottle for those "what ifs"
we go back and forth, and I forced you back and we've gotten so good at arguing
we go talk to text, then text to talk, then I'll hang up but you'll call again
then all your friends, I mean all your friends, all up in your ears, they talking and
you listen close and you call again to tell me what we had can't walk again...
...and you're gone.

Punch Drunk Mumbo

Answers in my mind
questions on my face
Feelings in my heart,
that I can't get away.
Sorrow found a spot
and Hope just gave its all
Love was right at home
but you forgot to call.
Thirty days you wander
and forty days I wait
I succumb to hunger
and turn to walk away.
I'm looking in your face
You're staring back at mine
staring at a ghost
Your eye has lost it's shine
...and every time I think about you in the moonlight
I think in thought that everything was just too right
and everyday I fight the feelings that aren't so nice
that all my fears are what you're feeding off in your nights.
but several times I came across you with no lights
to show you cared you sa

Marissa Lane

The pain in her tears me so
But how her love stirs
Like a breeze to the fire.
Oh I know, I know, yes I know
It's not fair.
I could see her getting tired.
When her heart bleeds, she thinks I'm clean
Oh, Marissa Lane, how could I ever be so mean?
She always says she's okay, but yet she cries.
Open arms for embrace, she declines
I'll own each tear that she spills like cherry wine.
The tears I've caused
She cries on the arms of another.
Cause I couldn't bear it.
The heart I once held
I long for the way to repair it.
Like rest for the weary
And she's worth it, at least to me
Oh Marissa Lane, don't clear your heart of me..
She still says she's okay, but how she cries.
Standing room for embrace, she declines.
I'll own each tear she spills like cherry wine.
Fight and fight she fights it
But true love will win,
Like breath to the living.
Sweet and calm and peaceful
Though she wants no more
Her heart is forgiving.
I won't give her up, but it's time.
Marissa Lane will live forever in my mind.
I know now that she's okay when she cries
I'll be here for embrace through declines
I've owned each tear she's spilled like cherry wine.
FIN

Ann Elise

She was my flower and I was deliberate as not to be selfish.
I knew that if I plucked her stem and brought her home
To be admired, that eventually she'd only die.
But that's what she wanted.
That's what she knew. That's what she needed.
She didn't know that she was a flower.
She knew that she wanted to be loved.
She knew that she wanted to be admired.
If it meant that she had to die with me, so be it.
But I was deliberate.
I was careful.
I refused to be selfish.
...and that's how I lost her.

When Today Was Still Tomorrow

"I was supposed to see you last night,
But I hated it.
Not for the prospect of seeing you but for
The mere fact that the morning would surely come
And I would have to leave you.
I was supposed to kiss you last night,
But I hated it.
So I went to the only places I knew
That would not change come daybreak.
That way my special change stays ahead.
A future to look forward to and not
A memory to yearn for again.
I was supposed to hold you last night.
I didn't
And I hate it."

I Painted The Sky Blue

She doesn't know what to think
Because I show her love in a different format.
A love that isn't like her last.
Her last, well she just knew it was her last.
Half guarded, mostly afraid.
Self portraits tinted with different hues of blues.
I try to help her paint better pictures
But that's clearly all she knows.
She washes my canvas with the tears of her fears.
She doesn't want me because she doesn't
Know my kind of love.
Maybe one day she'll realize what I'm trying to give her.
Of course it'll be much too late for us, but just the same,
At least she'll know that she's known real love.

this love thing

And again, I came here knowing that I just
Don't know how this love thing works.
One I loved too close.
One I loved too far.
A few I loved here and there.
Once I loved from behind a glass.

supersaturated

Someone is looking...looking for you with words.
Words written with blood on pages riddled with tears,
captivated by your red dust. God knows.
Someone is looking for you, looking to love you.
I overheard it earlier.
I passed him on my way out. I know I can't be him.
Maybe I can come back as him. Maybe I can find you as him.
Maybe next time I'll be him and not me.
He'll love you with blood sweat & tears.
So will I.
Each word supersaturated with love.

The Idea

Maybe because I prayed for her.
Not really in the way you probably just thought of though.
Real prayers. Real words.
I said words from my heart to God's ears
But again, probably not in the way that you're thinking.
I already had her and I prayed for her.
I begged for her, I pleaded.
Almost to the point of tears for her.
Yes, yes I prayed for her.
I prayed that I wouldn't be the man
To break her heart.
I prayed to know what to say to keep her smile.
I probably prayed for something impossible too.
I never thought it would last too long
So I prayed that while it did, I made her happy.
Hell, I tried. I tried like shit.
That's what I hang my hat on.

Some Thing To Do

"What a wicked thing to do,
making me fall in love with you.
Then leave me to dream things,
things like life, but live without you."

"I just wished you'd seen the bigger picture."

Maybe

Maybe it's because I loved my first with all of me
        and she hurt me.
Maybe it's because I loved my next with all of me
        and she hurt me.
Maybe it's because I loved my last with all of me
        and she hurt me.
There's no maybe that I'll love you with what's left of me
        even if you'll hurt me...
My all will be yours to have.
That's about all I can promise.

How Old Is This Love?

No matter what I thought
I realized that I knew love but oh so wrong.
I know love in all its beauty and in all its greatness.
But I did not know love when love seemed absent.
When she does not call, do I know her love?
When she walks away, do I still know love?
Or do I leave as well?
Did I know love here or did I have the love
That I've had before give me hope again?

Next To Nothing

You wanted to go with the flow of the wild river rapids
And I wanted to let you
But I held you in my net in the attempt to
Guide you downstream.
All the while paying no attention to the hole in the net
That bore from you weight.

Expectant

Expectant, I extended to you and I became expectant.
I wanted it in return, I wanted your heart.
Not only your heart, but your body and mind with it.
I wanted your love.
Not only your love but your desires and wishes with it.
I was encompassed in your rapture.
I fell. So…just oh so deep. Hell, I noticed it too later.
Now look at me…just look at me.
Alone.
Bitter. I'm fucking bitter and it's because I was so damn
Expectant. I extended to you and I became expectant.
I let myself be vulnerable…and look what that left me.
Expectant and alone…oh so alone.
Oh, but next time I'll know my lesson.
I'll never let another close. That'll teach you.
That'll be my new thing. I'll show you something new.
I'll be unfair to them to repair my expectancy for you.
Dammit.
I could never…I'll be expectant if it'd find me love.
I'll be expectant if it'll make you smile.
I'll be expectant if I'll get a chance.
I'll be expectant because that's all I know.
I'll plant my expectancy and water it with pain and hope that it grows.
Shit.

Teach me to fall. I'm tired of holding on to hope and I'm starting to feel weak.

All of Your Words

Because every time I see you, I see you in dreams.
Far off dreams.
Dreams that are the results of work, effort, love and caring.
Dreams that I'm determined to bring into fruition.
Because every time I saw you I sat up straight.
Because when I saw you I felt like I owed you more.
I know I owe you the whole of everything.
So much I want to attain just for you.
So much I want you to see my progression of life.
Oh so much.
And this tough man was no more than a handful of clay.
And the every time I'd take a knee and speak to my maker
I'd beg him to give me the power to make you happy.
Maybe he gave me that power and I'm just too much of
A man to understand it.
Because every time I saw you I saw you in dreams.
Dreams that I could control. Dreams that I could love.
And when you used all of you words I knew
I

Pillow Thoughts

It's her pleasure. It's her happiness.
It's her smell. It's her success.
It's her smile. It's her trust.
It's knowing that I can be responsible for it.
It's knowing that, for a fact, I know a thousand others that want her.
It's know that I know someone that would treat her just as good.
It's knowing that even with all this she chooses to be here.
She chooses to be with me.
She holds my heart in her hands and she could crush me.
She may never understand her power.

Sunrise Opera

I wake one eye opened
then I rub the other to get focused.
As I face this sunrise opera
I must search for my companion.
There you are right where I left you
for my slumber in the night,
and this time stolen between us was by a Thief that we call sleep
He tells me to treasure all the times I am awake with you.
So I sit up to greet the morning,
before my eyes could reach the window
I glance back at you to see
if you were awake yet to join me.
And the solemnest and solitude let's me appreciate
All His Mightiest creations in this sunrise opera bliss.

Where We Are

she's good for playing games, she wants to make up number names
and wants to be my Number One, if I won't be too ashamed
I say I want to be Eleven, and you can be my top five
plus six and seven ate nine, and I stay beside a dime
she loves my thoughts and wants to know what's on my mind
I live on Suicide Drive, baby girl I think I'm dying
cause I'm just killing myself the way I'm thinking bout you
and I'll tell you everything just give me a minute or two
baby you're perfect like the spring, you make me want to sing
and I couldn't carry a tune if I wrapped it with a string
could you do something with me? in lieu of something risky
 let me make love to your heart, so when I leave you can miss me
but I'm never gone too far, and I promise I'll be right back
and every time you hit me with a text, promise I'll write back
then right back and forth we can go until you're screaming...
please don't wake me if I'm dreaming...
  ...I'll see you in the morning.

Sunshine

never met her before, but I might
have to use her influence in whatever I write.
cant use mediocre to express my pleasure,
her eyes are like spring, her voice is like heaven.
her hair is like weather, fresh kissed by the sun,
her touch is like clouds, her laugh is like fun.
her lips are softer than anything I knew,
and her skin is every perfect shaded earth tone hue.
conquistador, I feel the need to conquer her heart
first name is May We, last name is Never Part
oh boy, I'm in trouble, these words I can't keep
I'll swim in her thoughts because man she's that deep
her smile calms a war, her will parts a sea
her jokes made me strong, her kiss makes me weak
her love is pure like first snow in December
heredity paid off, I think I found me a winner
you're my sunshine.

One Day Monday

Your scent, I wore your scent on me that day. I wore your scent around as though I had it bottled and shipped to me in its physical form. I thought of you every time the wind would shift and boy did the wind shift a lot that day. You sang to me before you left, I still catch myself humming that little tune. It's amazing how much I don't even like that silly little song, how terribly orchestrated I felt the lyrics were, how annoying the chorus could be, how off key the singer was when she'd sing, how beautifully you'd make it sound in your angelic voice. That voice of yours could calm a sea or tear through a building like a raging tornado. My goodness how I miss you coming over to visit. True you'd only be able to come by once a week, but that day spent with you was so much better than any other day. Honestly, the only way I really made it through the rest of the week is because I knew that once it was over I'd have you back again. Smiling to myself now just thinking of the way you'd furrow your brow when you'd try to be mad at me. We could never seem to get mad at each other even when we tried. In my defense though, who could get mad at a face like yours? You know I've never called you beautiful because you are beauty itself, personified. If you saw you through my eyes...but you hear that all the time, I'm not trying to flatter, I'm just passing compliments where they are due. I remember we'd walk together in a store and when people would ask your name I'd tell them all the same line that you hated..."I don't know what you should call her, but I call her Mine." I always thought that was cute, no clue why you don't like that. Your name is what did it for me anyway, I can't have every Joe in town knowing who you are Ms. Freeme...Monday S. Freeme, now that's what I look forward to once a week. Your scent Ms. Freeme, I wear your scent on me this day. I'm wearing your scent around because I bottled it myself in its physical form. I took your scent and sent it around the world twice and I brought it right back and I'm wearing it now. Your song Monday, I'm singing your song today. I'm singing every word today because I found that terrible little singer and I had her teach me every lyric. I had her teach me every lyric so that I could sing this song everyday. My brow My Love, my brow is as furrowed as I can stand. I furrow my brow My Love every time my lip shakes because that's the best thing I can do. You died and left me here to remember you. Just as I promised on that day I promise on this day to remember you and one day Monday I'll see you again. I love you.

Our Race

Who gave you permission to love me?
I never said it was okay.
Set me free to move
Though, I will not run.
I will love you until eternity is old.
Until I have loved a million leagues over,
and than the sun I am older,
I will not run.

St. Tirf

I haven't been in love for a long time,
now I'm knee deep in like, and its reaching up my thigh.
wrapping round my waist, I guess its heading for my heart
I'm not trying to fight it off, I guess I'm heading for a start
I mean is it worth it, O St. Tirf it's
kind of like I want her, but I know I'm not perfect.
Now I feel like the luckiest fellow, she's so mellow
I could swear I hear cellos, every time she says hello.
I mean when we're together I still miss her
her perfect earth tone is still softer than a whisper
I still go swimming in her thoughts when I kiss her
but I could only wish her, to be my own...
so for now I'll just stand in the cold, won't lose faith
watching through the windows of her soul, the views great
I know this one is one that's still worth a chase
Destiny and Fate told me slow down and wait
...for my sunshine.

"she may not be the best, but she's the best that I care to know."

Napkins

Wrote my feelings down on a napkin as I thought 'em
Then I folded up my napkin and I stuck it in my pocket
As I walked along so happy, couldn't wait until I saw you
But some dirt got in my eye and I cried before I caught you
My jacket was so dirty and my fingers wasn't working
So i grabbed the napkin, folded back the words and got the dirt
Then I placed it back not battered, kind of damp but nothing tattered
And I bopped along just singing kicking dirt as pigeons scattered
...dialing till my cell dies I'm trying to ring your hook off
the things I think about you I could probably write a book off
she doesn't have a flaw and I don't care what any dude says
I know you from afar because the bottoms of your shoes red
Saw a woman that I know I'll need to call her later
But my cell is dead, she has a pen but couldn't find her paper
So my napkin's what I pull out, fold back the words that stood out
I told her thanks and gave a hug and promised that I would shout
So I saw you minutes later, in my hand you saw the paper
I was waiting for your smile, but you started making faces
I guess you saw the name and number and you went ahead and lost it
Grabbed my napkin, ripped it up, then you spit on it and tossed it
Never mind to ask a question, you expect your heart to break
Her name was Alice and I know her from the Jewelry Store Exchange
See, I bought your wedding ring, I was gonna pick it up today
If you took the chance to wait, that's just what the napkin said...

My Heart

If you have love ever you want to hide
I have a place best kept a secret as ever
Oh this place I yearn to tell you of
Oh this place I yearn to tell you of
I have this place that has been tested.
Tested by the best battles known to gods
Gods of man and gods of gods
The light of heaven may not reach this place
just you speak the word...
Had you one choice to hide your love
Let me know, I shall give no clue to the opposition
I wont fan the flame
I shall let the smoke die if it shall take such.
My heart will go through hell to get to high water
My heart is where you will visit to find your love.
My heart is where I will keep you forever.
Forever.

Monarch

You crawled to me and I loved you unconditionally
I sheltered you clothed and cloaked you
I showed you what should be
And I tell you what could be
God knows I wanted you to believe it would be.
You grew in me, and we grew to be we
And just as your wings began to sprout
You were shoved from me
Moved from me, and I knew it was in me to be
Just to be enough of a man to let you be
I had to let you so that I may grow in me too
The most beautiful butterfly emerges yet from a caterpillar
The most wonderful flight emerges
It emerges from the most failed attempts
I love you
Blossom and spread your beauty

Freezing Hot

She telling me she loves me and not even trying to fake
Says she's ready for a wedding, she just trying to find a date
I'm not ready for a wife, I'm just trying find a date
I'm here searching for a friend, I'm not trying to find a mate
And I know you lying...wait, you should stop just lie and wait.
Girl you know I'm Lian Waite, my heart heavy like lion weight
Not trying defy fate, we should start out wit a greeting
I see that you know my name, but its only our first meeting
And its...checks and balances to find out what my balance is
And the real challenge is, will you be there through challenges?
When my...cash gets low will you let the door hit ya?
Or help write a rhyme because you can see the bigger picture?
Until then baby girl, let's take a couple steps slower
My mama said "don't get married son, until you really know her."
So take my number, send me a text and I promise I'll write back
Oh yea, what's your name? Oh really...? Yea, I like that.

Hope's Diamond

I've been mining this forever, I'll be shining this forever
if each moment were a raindrop, shower me forever.
Consider myself clever, I would follow you to heaven
or hell if you take me, your love just outweighs me
so now I pray to God you pray to God and not Satan
and I shall leave you "nevermore" if I could quote the raven.
Place your heart on a cloud and baby I'll go climbing
for my personal prized possession, my Hope Diamond.
I fell in love with your eyes and your lips blew me
I'd wait in line a lifetime just to glimpse your beauty.
If you promised me that you'd love me till time was up
I'd swear that my forever wasn't time enough.

Digital Girl

Wifi love baby, no strings needed
Here's a zip file wit my heart, you keep it
Put your iPhone down, no time for tweets
Facebook status update: "face beat"
Your ex all in your DM's asking "do you miss me"
Control "H" his ass, delete that history
Control alt delete, reset to another
Screensaver refresh, select "no suckers"
Now her service trash, just roaming on that ass
She can't even upload a damn dubsmash
Netflix just can't locate a server
Now she on LinkedIn, she hasn't been working
Free credit report dot com she can't login
Camera won't work so no video blogging
Text me caps locked, punctuation all random
Talking bout her ex loves and how she just can't stand em
...got no man but gonna get one though.
I write her love songs on my Samsung Note
you just might have a virus in that file named "Chatter"
Digital or analog, you're mine, it don't matter.

Do You Think About Me?

think about pain when you think about me
the only thing you'll never see when you hang around me
got the sun in the sky, hand in hand on the beach
you know I'll be your umbrella if the sun should ever weep
and you know I gotcha back when the sun goes to sleep
they call it nighttime, I call it special time for you and me
if a rumor's going around, then I promise I haven't heard it
you're the thing that comes to mind when I think about perfect
I think about leaving here and going overseas
so I can think of you in languages I couldn't even speak
I think about you more, you're the one that I adore
making love on the floor or the threshold of the door
on the balcony, the terrace, f*ck that mirror, you're the fairest
taking trips out to Paris, on the plane, let em hear us
put you and me together and I think you got "oui"
I always think about you, do you think about me...?

More

Souls lost don't know of your love
Your love is the kindest I have met yet
I speak in tongues and these tongues speak short
Words have not been created to describe what I feel
I feel only magic
Each day I see you anew
I could live each new day forever.
I could not move on, I could live on no long road to another
However long or short
I could never love another as such
I write to you with no regret
Your love is the best yet.

Because It's Thursday

she asks me is there a reason why I'm smiling, and I take a minute to reply like......
"baby I'm not smiling, I'm looking at tomorrow, because that's what I see in your eyes."
and she's not used to those truths because it all sounds too right, so she chalks it as games or lies
and the lonely girl inside her wants to believe that its all true, you know, everything that I say
and that what I say today will be what I say another day...a year from now.
but see, she got that fear from now...on out, that I will just fill her wit more pretentious bullshit
and then I'm gonna set her up and pull shit out of left field like, I don't want you...but she's my Love.
and she draws conclusions like she's thinking with a pen, i have to beg her don't confuse me
I'm not those other men and all those men are in your past so its apparent they were weaker
my expectations may be meager but what i expect from myself is oh so grand
I'll earn the right to be your man hand in hand, and this I demand of me
I want you to know that I can hear your soliloquy, stars will shine tonight just for you and me
and I cant promise you eternity, but I will say that all that I'm not I can learn to be
and wherever you fail or falter just know that you can always turn to me
I can be...no My Love, I will be everything you've always dreamed of...
and I give to you beyond what I even have the means of, you deserve it.
I just want you to know that that's the minimum of all the things that you're worth
and don't compare yourself to anything you've seen, you're more than this earth
so as you ask me for a ride, don't get mad when I ask where you're going
you know we can spend a lifetime not knowing, but now in your eyes I see your ambition showing
so don't question my motives as my smile starts growing, its your sweet love that I'm tasting
moments like this I'd spend a lifetime chasing, men yearn for this and lifetimes get wasted

so CLAP, CLAP, I give you standing ovation and BRAVO, and I tell you pray for next week
but live like there's no tomorrow, I promise I can only promise that these words aren't hollow
and maybe my last name one day would be something you'd consider, if your love is a jewel
I wouldn't mind being just that much richer, being that much closer and that much witcha.
because you inspire me to be a higher me, and I want to help you be all that you aspire to be
so smile with me, because its Thursday, the first day of forever, never let me hear you say never
unless its ¨never hurt me, never leave me ¨or ¨I'll never deceive thee¨ okay well then...
something of that nature, because no matter where you are in life you can always be greater
not saying this because it rhymes though sometimes even I feel like it may be sort of out of season
but all in all the simple answer is..."yes baby girl, I'm smiling for a reason."

I Hope You Don't Mind

Time heals wounds, but sometimes wounds don't heal with time.
Sometimes, some things are instilled deep in your heart or in your mind,
Where forgetfulness doesn't visit and crying just never reaches.
Sometimes, the best lessons you learn are the ones nobody teaches.
If you look to gauge your future by what your past becomes
You'll be the first to lose even though you are the last to run.
Now the things you think you're thinking, are the things you thought before,
Because you didn't have a clue what this love thing had in store
So you cry when no one listens, and hurt where no one sees,
How can you fail yourself when you're the only one to please?
So forget me slowly but remember who is always there
When no one else supports you and no one else really cares.
All you claim you want is love and so that you can be yourself,
All I have to offer is that and someone you can call for help.
When your heart is kind of hurting or it's not in the best of shape
Take a moment to reach out for me, there's no time that's too late.
I'll be here to hear your silence, or your pillow over the phone
Save your tears for something special you don't have to sing alone.

Baneke

i'd never want you there for me like im there for you, cuz im sure id get sick of you being around.
id love to give you the sky, but for now all i can afford is the ground.
id pull down a cloud to soften each step you'd make
each time you hurt that pain i'd take
that burden i'd carry, that hurt i'll bare
i'd bottle sunshine to wash your hair
i want to spend all my time with you, but be damned if i dont have to sleep.
i'd give you a star for no reason if God gave me one to keep.
and my new favorite color is all you are
i'd live once twice if i have your heart.
im so sick of dreaming and comin up bland, so ill meet you over halfway with my effort in hand.
all for my Baneke.

A4 Effort

Heaven's effort helped me put this into script and for you
and I want you for myself though I'm so nondescript towards you
and the every time I see you or we have our conversations
you see my cool exterior but inside I'm so elated.
I'm sure its not a secret, yea I hear what all is mentioned
I hear what people say, they know I'm loving your dimensions
I smile at your description, and I'm so in love with your ambitions
I'm tryin to join your campaign if you'd just sign my petition...(lol)
now the only thing I'm missing in my life see, is a wifey
or a woman to hold me down, I need a Queen to wear that crown
get your heels lets run the town, no attention to that extra bull
I swear my words are genuine, not derived of everything sexual
but please don't get me wrong, I imagine that being so pleasurable
but only in due time, right now I'm trying to read your mind
right now I'm trying to make you mine, hoping that you are my destiny
and anything that happens after that we can just let it be...

Shirts With Pockets

against my face, it's not perfect but that's the all that I have
against my face, place your hand against my face
feel my joy, my pleasure, my pain.
give me amnesty. amnesty from all that I will do.
kiss away the past, and welcome the future.
your kiss tastes of nothing. or at least nothing that I know.
new love. at least for one moment, and one moment again, and
one moment again, but pronounced with pro and proper nouns.
you've already stopped time, you need not worry now, Father Time himself
grows old waiting to begin again. for one moment again, and one moment
again
I hold you. I think of all the times we have been together...even at initial
meeting.
I've met you for the first time again, and my it is magnificent.
as miserly as I am, this love is my food. my drink. my wealth.
for one moment again, I am as a King...please My Love, against my face.
hold your lips against my face.
let not a tear dare dream to peer through your souls windows.
clinch tight now My Love, hold fast your heart and mind.
hold fast my heart as well, it is no longer my own. for one moment again...
just one moment again I sat in the hallways of love with you and discussed
my truths.
against my heart, though tattered and torn and badly bruised My Love
against my heart, hold my truths.
against your heart, though tattered and torn and badly bruised from Love
against your heart, hold my own

10:30 am

10:30 am
She is to me as a breath
As necessary, as concrete, as elusive.
I hold on as long as I can. I hold on for life.
I hold on true and I hold on tight.
Knowing all too well that she is a breath
And like a breath I'll have to let her go.
She will be mine as long as I hold her,
But she is still as free as a breath.
I'll hold her as long as I can and then...
...and then I'll set her free. I'll ser her free
To return to give me life. Life sustained. Life fulfilled.
And each day I'll set her free because this, yes this
This is my favorite part of her. Her return.
Her want. Her need. Her love. Her heart. Her pleas.
My love plans to love her love until her love won't love me.
And then again, and then again, I'll breather.
That great breath that is her.
And she'll fill me with herself as I fell her with me.
Knowing that I'm living on the hope.
That when I breather she returns.
Without my breath I just.
10:38 am

I Believe In Fears

My footprints left in the sand...
I look back and just before the tide washes
She steps in the same specific places.
I remember how close we were.
I remember how afraid I was.
I remember the look on her face.
I remember how it all felt.
I remember falling in love with her right there on the beach.
Waking before my alarm...
I look over and just at the end of my pillow
She sleeps in almost the same particular space.
I remember how beautiful she was.
I remember how terrified I was.
I remember how long I laid and stared at the perfection that is her.
I remember falling in love with her right there moments before my alarm blared for work.
One conversation under the stars about life...
I look over at her because my words escape me.
That's when I see that she catches the glimmer of hope on my face.
I remember how loud my silence spoke to her.
I remember how frightened her awareness left me.
I remember falling in love with her right there on a cold blanket under that Virginia sky.
Adjusting the lapel flower of my best man...
I look back and just past the onlooker's smiles and tears
I see her walking towards me one more time.
I remember how bad my anxiety was killing me.
I remember falling in love with her right there in front of everyone that could see it already.

Anastasia

Selfish and I need you
I'm a slave to your touch.
I need it like prescriptions
It's said I'm addicted
But they think too little of you
Because you're my religion.

I inhale you exhale me
I'm exactly where I need to be
Wrapped up in your flesh.
I begged for it
Now I'll explore it
Leave me here if I belong

That's Her

At the end of my grip, yep, that's her.
In my seemingly endless midday daydreams, that's her.
First text message, last phone call.
The one my mother asks about more than me, yep, that's her.
That smile on my face. These words on my page.
That perfume in the air, my whispers, my stare, that's her.
Thoughts. Dreams. Hope. Wishes. Endless ambition. Passion. Sex. Love.
Friendship, that's her. That's her. That is her.
She is love, from every tangled hair on her head
Right down to the toenail polish she applied just before bed.
She is the harbinger for the coming of joy.
My pleasure. That's her. My delight. My comfort. That's her.
My fears and my intent. That's her. She is life. She is breath.
My Lover.
That's her.

It's More

So, there was this smile...
...and I found joy in it.
She was, no I apologize, she is everything that beauty defines.
And I see her in the breeze.
And I hear her in the birds in the trees.
And I pray of me, but for her.
I pray that I won't fumbler her heart.
She recognizes that I am just a man. She knows.
Even though my every thought is her. In me she grows.
She is every favorite handwritten letter in the book of me.

The Funny Thing Is That I Could Name This Anything

Not even in my wildest dreams
Not even in the most distant remnants of a thought
Not ever. No chance.
There just could be no way I could imagine
meeting someone as powerful as you.

2,121

I thought of you today.
you were wearing nothing but your clothes.
well, that and a smile.
none of those worries that bothered you all week.
you didn't have any of those with you.
none of those problems. none of the drama.
none of the extra padding, none of the extra weight.
maybe you were happy to see me.
maybe you could tell how happy I was to see you.
I told you that today you didn't have to fight through anything.
I told you I'd take that battle for you today. I think you liked that.
you smiled a bit more. you looked like you were thinking of something
but you said it was nothing too big really...and you smiled again.
well...it was all just a thought. a pleasant thought.
come to think of it, that smile you wore looked a lot like
the one you're wearing now.

Colour

Green, her favorite color is green.
Well I wish I was Green.
Not an adjective, but a noun, like things.
She loves bright green
Like grass in spring.
I fear now she loves Green
More than she loves me.
So instead of Green, now I'm feeling Blue
Not sky, but more of an ocean hue.

"let's visit all the places that important people sing about."

10,957

...that's a lot of days, and as of today that's my current count. I'm not sure which one of those days I realized how important growing in confidence is to your soul, but one day I woke up like..."shit I can do anything, except make a white baby." That makes me feel good. That's what goes through my mind when there's something new to me that I want to accomplish. It excites me to fill another void in my banks of knowledge and learn and grow. I'm growing older and I don't mind it because there's only one way out of getting old and I have too much living to do for that. So I guess I'm onto a new chapter in my life and all that jazz. My favorite saying when you're faced with a task that may be a bit much..."people do it all the time, right?" I'm thankful for my first 10,957 and here's to another 20k...

About The Author

My given name is Robert D. Urquhart Jr. I love my friends like family and my family more than myself. I just want to be someone that you'd be proud to know.

Also, I think this photo is funny.

Bare With Me

3/5	76
3AM in Liansburg	48
A Beggars Requiem	33
An Alpine Pioneer	32
A Piece of Quiet	84
A Red Harry	27
Be More	75
Blank Canvas	68
Breakfast	36
Cake	37
Chance	67
Cloudy With A Chance…	34
Congraduations !!!!	35
David The Goliath	15
da Vinci's "David"	73
Dear Woman	82
Dieu Noir	38
Forever	39
For Tami	17
Gateway Drug	40
Geisha	57
Govt. St & Cherry Ave	61
Graphic Design	28
Greener Pastures	14
Helen Back	26
Henry I Valentine	69
Her.	85
Heroes & Heroine	70
hisstory	58
…in a sad	31
…in my mind	29
I Prey	18
It's A New Year	64
Jutes For Scenes	42
Lecture	43
Mama Math	16
March Eighteen	19
Mood	78
Monedays	79
Mother's Day Poem	20
Mr. Pilfer	44
No Working Title	12
Opus Doe	45
Oui	71
Part of You	21
Past My Shades	47
Photo Racers	63
Pompous	50
Real Orange Peelings	22
Remember	23
Runway 6	56
Shelf of Steam	55
Sicks Menits Lian Waite	54
Teddy's Diary	25
Terrorist	46
The Breakup	53
The Great Escape	41
The Last, Last	62
The Moment	51
The Silence of Forever	81
Thought Process	52
titled	80
Today's Date	24
Tokyo Grey	13
Within	65
Woman	83
Work	66
write then, write away	49
Write up	60
Young Love	72

I'm Terrible With Names

"VI"	94
10:30am	141
2,121	147
10,957	150
A4 Effort	139
All I Want Is You	101
All Of Your Words	118
All Over Diane	102
Anastasia	143
Ann Elise	105
Baneke	138
Bang! Went My Shooter	100
Because It's Thursday	135
Burnt Glass	99
Colour	148
Digital Girl	132
Do You Think About Me?	133
Driftin' On By	95
Ears Full of Tears	97
Expectant	116
First Grade	96
Freezing Hot	130
Hope's Diamond	131
How Old Is This Love?	114
I Believe In Fears	142
I Hope You Don't Mind	137
I Painted The Sky Blue	107
It's More	145
Marissa Lane	104
Maybe	113
Monarch	129
Monday Origami	91
More	134
My Heart	128
Napkins	127
Next To Nothing	115
One Day Monday	123
Our Race	124
Pillow Thoughts	119
Poems & Songs	92
Punch Drunk Mumbo	103
Shirts With Pockets	140
Snow Days	88
Some Thing To Do	111
St. Tirf	125
Sunrise Opera	120
Sunshine	122
supersaturated	109
That's Her	144
The End	98
The Funny Thing Is...	146
The Idea	110
This Love Thing	108
When Today Was Still...	106
Where We Are	121

Acknowledgements

I was going to thank everyone that gave me inspiration here individually, but as you already know I'm terrible with names and I fear I'd forget someone. So what I'd like to do is thank you. You, my beloved reader friend, I want you to know how much I appreciate you. That's what means the most to me. Any and every one that took a moment out of their life to spend a moment in mine, thank you. However you happened across this collection whether you purchased, borrowed, rented, found, stole or overheard the book from someone else, I appreciate you. From the bottom of my heart, thank you so much for your time, love and patience with me.

Lian Waite

FIN.

www.ingramcontent.com/pod-product-compliance
Ingram Content Group UK Ltd.
Pitfield, Milton Keynes, MK11 3LW, UK
UKHW041305180426
11947UKWH00009B/702